Selected Poems

Ausgewählte Gedichte

Selected Poems

Ausgewählte Gedichte

A Dual-Language Book

RAINER MARIA RILKE

Edited and Translated by
STANLEY APPELBAUM

DOVER PUBLICATIONS, INC.
Mineola, New York

Bibliographical Note

This Dover edition, first published in 2011, contains the full German text of 104 poems by Rilke, reprinted from standard sources (see the Introduction for specific data on the original volume publications, etc.), together with new English translations. Stanley Appelbaum made the selection, did the translations, and wrote the Introduction and the footnotes.

Library of Congress Cataloging-in-Publication Data

Rilke, Rainer Maria, 1875–1926.
  [Poems. English & German. Selections]
  Selected poems = Ausgewählte gedichte / Rainer Maria Rilke ; edited and translated by Stanley Appelbaum. —Dover ed.
     p. cm.—(A dual-language book)
  Text in both English and German.
  Includes index.
  ISBN-13: 978-0-486-47861-6
  ISBN-10: 0-486-47861-0
     I. Appelbaum, Stanley. II. Title. III. Title: Ausgewählte gedichte.
  PT2635.I65A17 2010
  831′.912—dc22   2010033096

Manufactured in the United States by Courier Corporation
47861001
www.doverpublications.com

CONTENTS

The numbering of the poems has been introduced in this Dover edition for convenience of reference.

v

Das Stunden-Buch / The Book of Hours

Das Buch der Bilder / The Book of Images

Neue Gedichte [Erster Teil] / New Poems [Part I]

Der neuen Gedichte anderer Teil / New Poems, Part II

Requiem / Requiem

Das Marien-Leben / The Life of the Virgin

Duineser Elegien / Duino Elegies

Die Sonette an Orpheus / The Sonnets to Orpheus

INTRODUCTION

Rilke's Life and Career

A biographer has said of Rilke: "His genius was the most consummate and his versatility the greatest of all the European poets writing in the years bordering 1900"; and many consider him to be the foremost German-language poet of the twentieth century.

René Karl Wilhelm Johann Josef Maria Rilke was born in Prague in 1875. Of lower-class Bohemian descent, he adopted his father's mythical belief in a noble, chivalrous ancestry (one wealthy uncle had actually been ennobled in 1873). The poet's father had had some military training and experience in his youth, but ended up as a solidly bourgeois railroad official, longing in vain to become an estate steward like his own father. The poet's mother, a banker's daughter, was a prideful, superficial, and religiously bigoted woman who overprotected her sickly boy and dressed him in girl's clothes till he was five, as a substitute for the daughter who had died a few days after birth.

Young René, who displayed early talents in drawing and verse composition, remained with his father after his mother deserted them in 1884 for the arms of a lover and the bright lights of Vienna (she and the poet met occasionally until 1915; she was to outlive him by five years). In 1886, after four years of primary school in Prague, René was packed off to a military academy in Sankt-Pölten (in Austria, west of Vienna), where he suffered from the vulgarity of his surroundings and his poor athletic showing.[1] In 1890 he spent his senior year at the

---

[1] His 1902 story "Die Turnstunde" (The Gym Class), recalling the hell he suffered at the academy, is included (along with stories mentioned later in this Introduction: "Die Weise von Liebe und Tod des Cornets Christoph Rilke" and all thirteen stories in the cycle *Geschichten vom lieben Gott*) in the Dover dual-language volume (same translator as this one) *Great Stories by Kafka and Rilke* (2003; ISBN 0-486-43197-5).

military academy at Mährisch-Weisskirchen in Moravia. In 1891 he entered business school in Linz (Austria), but was back in his native city the following year.

In Prague, his uncle made him an allowance and he received a good Gymnasium (classical secondary school) education from 1892 to 1895, publishing his first verse collection, *Leben und Lieder* (Life and Songs), in 1894. (In these years he had casual liaisons and was briefly engaged.) In 1895 and 1896 he attended Prague University, studying liberal arts and law, and mingling in the city's German-language literary circles. (German speakers were an isolated minority there, still artificially elevated socially, many as industrialists and traders, because Bohemia was still part of the Austro-Hungarian Monarchy, but becoming increasingly marginalized by the native Czechs. A sense of alienation is very strong, or latent, in the German writings of Rilke's contemporaries in Prague, such as Kafka, Meyrink, Werfel and Brod.)

Late in 1896, possibly embarrassed by the resounding failure of a play, Rilke moved to the great cultural center Munich, now convinced that he must commit himself to creative endeavors. There, in 1897, he met Lou Andreas-Salomé (1861–1937), the Russian-born wife of a German professor; she had already been a close friend of Nietzsche's and was later to be a valued associate of Freud's. Lou became Rilke's mistress and persuaded him to change his first name to the Germanic "Rainer." The poet followed her when she returned to Berlin in 1897 (the German capital was to remain his official domicile until 1900), and accompanied her on two trips to Russia, in the spring of 1899 and the summer of 1900. Russia was a decisive experience for him; he was thrilled by its wide open spaces, and touched by what he perceived as the simple pristine piety of the Russian peasant. After the second trip the liaison with Lou cooled, but they remained good friends and correspondents.

From 1900 to early 1902 Rilke lived near Bremen in northern Germany, specifically in Westerwede and in Worpswede, the artists' colony on the heath where in April 1901 he married the sculptress Clara Westhoff (1878–1954), a pupil of the great Auguste Rodin (1840–1917); the Rilkes' daughter Ruth was born in December 1901. The marriage was casual, in bohemian fashion, and after the poet moved to Paris in 1902 (the French capital would be the jumping-off place in his nomadic life until the outbreak of the First World War) Clara and Rainer met only from time to time, though remaining friends.

That move to Paris may have been occasioned by the poet's reflection that he ought to provide for his new family, his father being unable to support him any longer. At any rate, he had received a commission to write a monograph on Rodin; this was published in 1903, as was another, on Worpswede. (Rilke continued to write essays until 1921, published his major, and only nonjuvenile, novel in 1910, was an active translator from 1908 to 1925, and produced a voluminous correspondence, but his career as a playwright and writer of sketches and short stories—dating back to 1889—virtually ended in 1902. Thereafter he poured all his real creativity into his poetry, which is discussed at length later in this Introduction.)

Paris was another life-changing experience for Rilke; it was the biggest metropolis he had lived in, and he was deeply affected by the poverty and disease he saw there. A tourist since 1897, he now began a largely nomadic existence, visiting many parts of western Europe and even North Africa and Egypt. In 1904 he was in Scandinavia, probably doing research for his major novel about an artistically inclined young Dane in Paris, *Die Aufzeichnungen des Malte Laurids Brigge* (The Notebooks of M.L.B.). In parts of 1910, 1911, 1912, and 1914 he was the guest of the aging Princess Marie von Thurn und Taxis-Hohenlohe (1855–1934)—whom he had met in Paris in 1909—in her castle at Duino, on the Adriatic, west of Trieste.

During these prewar years Rilke was supported by his writings and his reading tours, but he also received subsidies from numerous patrons of the arts; some of his ladies-bountiful supplied other comforts as well. He lived for his art, avoiding serious attachments and regular employment, though he did handle Rodin's correspondence in 1905 and 1906. Rilke was an elegant, aristocratic, and somewhat precious cosmopolite.

At the outset of the war in 1914, when Rilke was in Munich, he was filled with his old, spurious martial ardor, but he soon recanted in view of the actual sordidness of events—especially when he was drafted into the Austrian home reserves in late 1915. Naturally, he was miserable there, even in the military records office. He was released after six or seven months, returning to Munich. But the end of the war saw the creation of an independent Czechoslovakia (no home for him) and a series of abortive revolutions in Germany, especially in Munich, where the centuries-old Wittelsbach dynasty crumbled. In 1919, after contracting for a reading tour in Switzerland, a country he had always affected to hold in contempt, Rilke began to look on the confederation as a new home.

There he was fortunate enough to meet and impress the four Reinhart brothers of Winterthur (a small town northeast of Zurich), who were wealthy international traders and patrons of the arts. Oskar Reinhart's art collection is still the pride of Winterthur. In 1921 Werner Reinhart (1884–1951), who financed Stravinsky's *L'histoire du soldat* in 1918, Honegger's *Le roi David* in 1921, and other musical and theatrical works with Swiss roots, rented for Rilke the small château that had caught the poet's fancy at Muzot in the Valais (the upper Rhône valley in French-speaking Switzerland).

At Muzot, in the *mensis mirabilis* of February 1922, Rilke, who had ostensibly "dried up" poetically, not having published any verse since *Das Marien-Leben* in 1913, produced the phenomenal outpouring of the *Duineser Elegien* and *Die Sonette an Orpheus* (see below). But by 1923 he was suffering from a rare form of leukemia, and he spent much of the rest of his life in clinics, dying in the clinic of Val-Mont, near Montreux, in 1926.

Bibliography

This new anthology includes at least one poem from every major subdivision of every volume of verse that Rilke personally saw through the press, except for the juvenilia he disowned: *Leben und Lieder* (Life and Songs; 1894) and *Wegwarten* (Wild Chicory; 1896). (He also wrote scores of poems, in German, French, and even Russian, that he didn't include in collections.) The sequence of volumes followed here is the one established in the *Sämtliche Werke* (Complete Works), Vol. 1, *Gedichte: Erster Teil* (Poems: First Part; Insel Verlag, Frankfurt am Main, 1955). Within each volume the poems appear here in their original order. The numbering of the poems from 1 to 104 has been introduced here for convenience of reference, and has no further validity. The selections range in length from six to 271 lines.

The volume *Erste Gedichte* (First Poems; a deliberate misnomer) was first published in 1913 by Insel Verlag, Leipzig. It comprised three earlier volumes: (i) *Larenopfer* (Offering to the Household Gods), published by Dominicus, Prague, at Christmas 1895; it was probably written in Prague in the late fall of that year; it didn't indicate dates of composition for the individual poems; it is the ultimate source of our poem 1. (ii) *Traumgekrönt* (Crowned with Dreams), published by P. Friesenhahn, Leipzig, December 1896; the poems in it were written between 1894 and 1896; it is the ultimate source of our poem 2, which was written in Prague on Sept. 22, 1896. (iii) *Advent,* published by Friesenhahn at Christmas 1897; the poems in it were written in 1896 and 1897; it is the ultimate source of our poem 3, written in Prague on September 7, 1896.

Die frühen Gedichte (The Early Poems) was published in May 1909 by Insel Verlag, Leipzig. It was a revised and slightly enlarged version (Rilke did the revision in 1908 and 1909) of the volume *Mir zur Feier* (Celebrating Myself), published by Georg Heinrich Meyer, Berlin, at Christmas 1899, and containing poems written in 1897 and 1898. *Die frühen Gedichte* is the source of our poems 4–10. Individual dates of composition (4–8 written in Berlin; no places and only conjectural dates for 9 and 10, which didn't appear in *Mir zur Feier):* 4: Jan. 8, 1898. 5: Feb. 8, 1898. 6: Nov. 19, 1897. 7: Nov. 21, 1897. 8: Feb. 6, 1898. 9: Ca. 1900? 10: 1898 or 1899?

Das Stunden-Buch (The Book of Hours) was published at Christmas 1905 by Insel Verlag, Leipzig. The poems in it were written in 1899, 1901, and 1903, and were revised in April and May of 1905. The book, from which our 11–28 are taken, is in three main sections: (i) "Das Buch vom mönchischen Leben" (The Book of Monastic Life), written in Berlin in September and October of 1899, revised at Worpswede, 1905; the source of our 11–18. Individual dates of composition: 11 and 12: September 20, 1899. 13–15: September 22, 1899. 16: September 24, 1899. 17: September 26, 1899. 18: October 1, 1899. (ii) "Das Buch von der Pilgerschaft" (The Book of Pilgrimage), written in Westerwede, September 18–25, 1901; revised in Worpswede, April and May of 1905; the source of our 19–25. Individual dates of composition: 19 and 20: September 18, 1901. 21: September 19, 1901. 22: September 20, 1901. 23: September 21, 1901. 24: September 22, 1901. 25: September 24 and 25, 1901. (iii) "Das Buch von der Armut und vom Tode" (The Book of Poverty and Death), written in Viareggio, April 1903; revised in Worpswede, April and May of 1905; the source of our 26–28. Dates: 26: April 13, 1903. 27: April 14, 1903. 28: April 19 and 20, 1903.

Das Buch der Bilder (The Book of Images) was published July 1902 by Axel Juncker, Berlin; the same publisher issued a second, enlarged edition (with 37 more poems) in December 1906. The first edition included poems written between 1898 and 1901; the 1906 additions were written between 1902 and 1906. Rilke made a final revision for the 1913 fifth edition. *Das Buch der Bilder* is the source of our poems 29–47 (29–35 are from the First Part of the First Book; 36–41 are from the Second Part of the First Book; 42–44 are from the First Part of the Second Book; 45–47 are from the Second Part of the Second Book). Individual places and dates of composition: 29 and 31: Berlin, July 22, 1899. 30: Berlin, July 24, 1899. 32: Meudon, written 1905–1906. 33: Berlin, Mar. 21, 1900. 34, 36, 37: Probably Paris, 1902–1903. 35: Paris, May 1903. 38: Paris, September 21, 1902. 39. Jonsered (near Göteborg, Sweden), ca. November 1, 1904 (prepublished in a longer version in the fall of 1905). 40: Perhaps Sweden, fall of 1904; at any rate, between 1902 and 1906. 41: Berlin, October 1900. 42: Berlin, July 28, 1899. 43: Written on two occasions—the first part in Worpswede, October 1, 1900; the second part, beginning "So wurden," Berlin, April 12, 1900. 44: Probably Rome, in the winter of 1903–1904. 45: Berlin, Nov. 14, 1900. 46: Berlin, Jan. 1901. 47: Probably 1900–1901 (prepublished in Vol. III of *Avalun*, 1901).

What was to be the first part of *Neue Gedichte* (New Poems) was published in December 1907 by Insel Verlag, Leipzig; it contained poems written between 1903 and 1907; it is the source of our poems 48–70. Individual places and dates of composition: 48: Paris, July 11, 1906. 49: Capri, Mar. 1907. 50: Meudon, winter of 1905–1906. 51 and 53: Paris, May–June of 1906. 52: Paris, June 1906. 54: Capri, Mar. 1907. 55: Paris, July 1907. 56: Paris, 1903 or late 1902 (prepublished, Sept. 1903). 57 and 58: Same as 50. 59: Paris, July 1906. 60 and 61: Same as 52. 62: Probably Paris, spring 1906. 63: Same as 49. 64: Paris, July 1906. 65 and 66: Same as 52. 67 and 69: Rome, early 1904, and Jonsered, fall 1904. 68: Capri, Feb. 1907. 70: Capri, early 1907.

Der neuen Gedichte anderer Teil (New Poems, Part Two) was published in November 1908 by Insel Verlag, Leipzig; it contained poems written between July 1907and August 1908; it is the source of our poems 71–88. Individual places and dates of composition: 71: Paris, summer 1908. 72: Either Paris, fall 1907, or Capri, spring 1908. 73: Paris, Aug. 1907. 74: Paris, Aug. 21, 1907. 75: Paris, summer 1908. 76 and 77: Paris, Aug.–Sept. of 1907. 78: Same as 74. 79 and 80: Same as 75. 81 and 82: Same as 72. 83: Paris, Aug. 3, 1907. 84: Same as 72. 85: Paris, Aug. 2, 1907. 86: Same as 72. 87: Same as 75. 88: Same as 76 and 77.

The volume *Requiem*, consisting of two long poems, is reprinted in its entirety here. It was published in May 1909 by Insel Verlag, Leipzig. Our poem 89 was written in Paris between Oct. 31 and Nov. 2, 1908. Poem 90 was written in Paris on Nov. 4 and 5, 1908.

Das Marien-Leben (The Life of the Virgin), the source of our 91–94, was published in June 1913 by Insel Verlag, Leipzig; it was No. 43 of their series "Insel-Bücherei"; the poems in it were written at Duino in January 1912, with the exception of poem 94, which was written in Nov. 1911 and revised in Jan. 1912.

Duineser Elegien (Duino Elegies) was published by Insel Verlag, Leipzig, in 1923 (limited edition in June, general edition in October); its ten poems were written between 1912 and 1922; it is the source of our poems 95–98. Individual places and dates of composition: 95:

Duino, Jan. 1912. 96: Duino, Jan. and Feb. of 1912. 97: Duino, Mar. 1912, and chiefly at Muzot, Switzerland, Feb. 9, 1922. 98: Duino, early 1912, and Paris, late 1913; revised at Muzot, Feb. 11, 1922.

Die Sonette an Orpheus (The Sonnets to Orpheus), a collection of 55 sonnets of varying line lengths, was published by Insel Verlag, Leipzig; both the limited and the general editions appeared in March 1923; the poems were written at Muzot between Feb. 2 and Feb. 23, 1922. Our poems 99–102 are from Part One; 103 and 104, from Part Two. Individual dates of composition: 99 (the original I, I): Feb. 2–5, 1922. 100 (I, VII) and 101 (I, IX): like 99, but revised Feb. 23, 1922. 102 (I, XXI): February 9, 1922. 103 (II, XII): Feb. 15–17, 1922. 104 (II, XXI): Feb. 17–23, 1922.

Commentary

Offered here are general comments on each individual volume (including dedicatees where applicable) and specific comments on a few of the individual poems. No identification is given for figures from the Bible or for the better-known aspects of classical mythology.

The *Erste Gedichte* are still thoroughly Neoromantic, but though somewhat conventional and derivative, they are charming and already exhibit Rilke's amazing technical proficiency.

The *Frühe Gedichte* tend to be more original, addressing the poet's personal concerns, such as his distrust of big cities and of the complacent bourgeoisie.

The *Stunden-Buch* is dedicated to Lou Andreas-Salomé, with whom Rilke made his two trips to Russia; and, indeed, as in the story cycle *Geschichten vom lieben Gott* (Stories About the Good Lord; 1900; revised edition, 1904), Russia was the poet's chief inspiration here. Some of the pieces are written in the persona of a Russian monk, and the book is tinged throughout by folk piety. A number of the poems examine the nature of God and his relationship to man in a decidedly non-Christian manner (Rilke had officially abandoned his childhood Catholicism, though it was to color his work all his life in subject matter and in attitude.) Unlike Rilke's later practice, he often lets his discourse here run on from one poem to another. Poem 16: The children's ball game of "catch" is alluded to here and in a number of Rilke's poems, all the way to the *Sonette an Orpheus*, almost as an idée fixe. Poem 28: The unnamed protagonist must be Saint Francis of Assisi (ca. 1181–1226); the mention of "brother" and "little flowers" substantiates this, as well as the cordial relationship with the "Poor Clares."

The *Buch der Bilder* is more of a miscellany, characterized by ever bolder imagery, and a little more density of expression, demanding the reader's full concentration. It reflects Rilke's life in Berlin and Worpswede, his early days in Paris, and his early travels in western Europe. Poem 34: Despite his unhappiness in military school and his utter incompetence as a cavalryman, here—as in poems 61–63 and his prose poem "Die Weise von Liebe und Tod des Cornets Christoph Rilke" (The Ballad of Love and Death of Cornet Christoph Rilke)— the poet indulges himself in dreams of martial glory and harps on his putative noble ancestry. Poem 38: The final stanza is very reminiscent of the poem "Vereinsamt" (Solitary) by the philosopher Friedrich Nietzsche (1844–1900). Poem 39: Skåne is the southwesternmost province of Sweden, close to Denmark. Poem 42: Pietrabianca is either a fictitious place, or else too small to figure even in multivolume Italian encyclopedias. The next-to-last line contains rampant synesthesia (Baudelaire-inspired): a fragrance is said to possess both color and sound. Poem 44: The Colonnas were one of the principal noble families in medieval and Renaissance Rome.

The enormously influential *Neue Gedichte* [Part One] was dedicated to Karl and Elisabeth von der Heydt; Karl (1858–1922) was a banker and writer; a patron of Rilke since 1905, he introduced the poet to many of the noble ladies who mothered him; Elisabeth (1864–1963) was Karl's wife. Part Two of the *Neue Gedichte* was dedicated to Rodin, whom Rilke credited as having imparted his work ethic to him. These volumes introduced Rilke's famous "objective poems" (*Dinggedichte*), coolly descriptive pieces in which personal emotions are kept under wraps (though hardly ever totally absent). Until his amazing *Duineser Elegien* and *Sonette an Orpheus* created new standards for comparison, the *Neue Gedichte* volumes probably represented the summit of the poet's achievement. Some of the poems can already be quite complex. They include ardent love songs, biblical paraphrases, numerous references to classical mythology, and many impressions of Parisian life. Poem 54: One of Rilke's major self-serving statements about the women in his life; despite the poem's title and form, it's hard to imagine the women themselves using such terms. For him, great art precluded lasting attachments, and here women (even if they supported him) are viewed as *le repos du poète*. Poem 56: In a letter of 1926, Rilke states that this poem (the earliest written in *Neue Gedichte*) was his first close observation of nature, after Rodin had taught him to be less superficial. The Jardin des Plantes (also mentioned in poems 82 and 86) was the major Parisian zoo in Rodin's day. The frequent repetition of the dull *ä*-sound in the first stanza reflects the monotony of the panther's life. Poem 58: The metaphor of a water bird that's clumsy on land is an unmistakable *hommage* to the poem "L'albatros" from the *Fleurs du mal* (1857) by Charles Baudelaire (1821–1867). Poem 59: "Tanagra" refers to certain terracotta figurines of the Hellenistic period, often depicting fashionable ladies. Poem 64: "Borghese" refers to the Villa Borghese, a major park in Rome. This poem is apparently a conscious variation on the famous poem "Der römische Brunnen" (The Roman Fountain) by the Swiss writer Conrad Ferdinand Meyer (1825–1898). Poem 65: The Jardin du Luxembourg is a popular Left Bank park in Paris. The repeated refrain suggests the endless rotation of the carousel. Poem 68: This piece was inspired by the play *Alcestis* (438 B.C.) by Euripides (480s–406). In a letter of 1907, Rilke says that the opening scene of this poem may have been his first attempt to use human beings as closely observed models, rather than flowers, animals, and landscapes. Poem 75: The Stylite is Saint Simeon Stylites (ca. 390–459), the Syrian Christian ascetic who spent 37 years atop a column. Poem 83: The "Montez" is most likely the outstanding Cadiz-born torero Francisco Montes, dubbed Paquiro (1805–1851). He was not yet prominent by 1830, and that date may possibly stand for the 1830s in general. Poem 86: Phryne was one of the most famous courtesans of ancient Greece, the mistress of the sculptor Praxiteles (he died in 390 B.C.). Poem 88: Rilke was impressed by what he knew of Islam, and particularly admired the Koran.

The two poems that comprise *Requiem* were written in memory of other creative people, but Rilke clearly uses himself as a model of the artist who must devote himself ruthlessly to his art, laboring incessantly to refine it while stoically ignoring the world's joys and pains, and never giving up (lessons he claimed to have learned from Rodin). (Of course, all of Rilke's works are basically about himself and express his own views, however much distorted by his background and his inclinations—a fact that, for instance, causes disappointment to dewy-eyed readers desirous of finding salubrious universal truths and guides to life in the *Duineser Elegien*.) Poem 89 is addressed to the wraith of Paula Becker (1876–1907), the most talented member of the Worpswede artists' colony. In 1901, after she rejected Rilke's proposal (they had met in 1900), he married Clara Westhoff and Paula married the local painter Otto Modersohn (1865–1943), calling herself Modersohn-Becker. The poem refers to her death in childbirth and to her paintings, still lifes and a seminude self-portrait in which she wears an amber necklace. Poem 90 is addressed to a young aristocratic poet, born 1887, who killed himself in 1906. He was not a close acquaintance of Rilke's, but the poem is quite the reverse of an indifferent, pious, commissioned chore!

Das Marien-Leben, probably Rilke's least interesting volume as a whole, though he applies his imagination to the old legends, was dedicated to Heinrich Vogeler (1872–1942), an artist and writer resident at Worpswede in Rilke's time (but he had first met Rilke in Florence in 1898); when Vogeler asked to illustrate some older works by Rilke, the poet decided to write this new cycle for him (though the volume was eventually published without illustrations). The superb German composer Paul Hindemith (1895–1963) set all fifteen poems in the cycle to music in two versions, 1924 and 1947. Poem 94: This poem, the earliest in the cycle to be written, was inspired by a Gothic image in the cathedral at Aquileia, Italy.

The celebrated volume *Duineser Elegien*, dedicated, though tacitly and not formally, to the princess who owned Duino, has been called "a metaphysics of consciousness" and "the most dramatic, albeit personally dramatic, work of this [the twentieth] century." Tinged with Expressionism, the language is demanding but only rarely hermetic. Among the topics are the pettiness of man in the universe, the enormous difficulties confronting love between man and woman, the threats to artistic creativity, the importance of intuition, and the constant seesawing between man's self-confidence and his insecurity in the world. Poem 95: Gaspara Stampa (1523–1553) was a Padua-born poet whose works often lament her lover's protracted absences. Linos is a vague, contradictory figure from Greek mythology (possibly based merely on a folk etymology) associated with Apollo and the Muses and with the origins of music in funeral laments. Poem 98: The *pschent* was the pharaonic crown symbolizing the union of Upper and Lower Egypt. The "mothers" probably refer to the mysterious chthonic powers mentioned by Goethe in both parts of *Faust* (1808 and 1832) on the basis of ancient Greek writings.

The *Sonette an Orpheus* volume bears the subtitle "Written as a Memorial Monument for Wera Ouckama Knoop." This young dancer (1900–1919) was the daughter of a writer, and her mother was one of Rilke's frequent correspondents. Critical words are inadequate to express the uncanny exuberance of these gemlike, oracular works in which the main aspects of the mythological figure of Orpheus are exploited: as a magical musician capable of charming the wild beasts, and as a knower, and thus partaker, of the two realms of the living and the dead (because of his attempt to bring his dead wife Eurydice back to earth from the underworld; compare poem 67). These pieces are Rilke's ultimate hymns to the creative artist. Poem 102: In a note to the *Sonette*, Rilke wrote that he was inspired by a children's chant he had heard in a convent in Ronda (Andalusia). The poem has the luminous simplicity of some of Mozart's late songs and operatic numbers, such as Papageno's arias in *The Magic Flute*. Poem 103: Rilke always made much use of alliteration, but here the repetition of W's helps to structure the entire poem.

The Nature of This Edition

It has been said of Rilke that he "explores the latent possibilities of the German tongue more fully than any poet before or after him." That alone would already make a translator's burden heavy, but in addition Rilke uses a recherché vocabulary including rare words, regional words, archaic words, words reserved for poetry only, words in peculiar guises, newly coined words, and polysemous words the appropriate meaning of which must be deduced from the context (if possible!).

Therefore, in a dual-language edition, with its pedagogical ends, it behooves the translator to eschew fancy trimmings and to hew as closely to the sense of each line as is consistent with proper, normal English. Thus, no attempt has been made to introduce regular meter and rhyme (this almost always either produces tinny jingles lacking the satisfying inevitability of Rilke's rhymes at their best, or necessitates padding with material not present in the original, or at times even results in verbiage that's harder to understand than the original!). Also avoided here is the tic that has affected some of the best English versions of Rilke: the arbitrary remaking of line breaks, usually resulting in more, and shorter, English lines. This Dover translation is doggedly line-for-line, except where the great differences between German and English syntax called for a redistribution of an utterance between two lines (this is frequent) or, very occasionally, over three or more. But, above all, the Dover translation strives to avoid the ambiguities, Germanisms, false cognates, and un-English word order characteristic of a few predecessors.

Many English-language translators have been tempted to try their skills and luck on Rilke (there has even been at least one team in which a writer innocent of German has worked with a "native informant"). One gratifying trait common to just about all of them has been a warm acknowledgment to those who have gone before. Let this worthy tradition not be broken here: this Dover translator, though often "begging to differ," owes many insights and enlightenments to the brave men and women who have led the way.

Selected Poems

Ausgewählte Gedichte

1. Der Novembertag

Kalter Herbst vermag den Tag zu knebeln,
seine tausend Jubelstimmen schweigen;
hoch vom Domturm wimmern gar so eigen
Sterbeglocken in Novembernebeln.

Auf den nassen Dächern liegt verschlafen
weißes Dunstlicht; und mit kalten Händen
greift der Sturm in des Kamines Wänden
eines Totenkarmens Schlußoktaven.

2. "Schon starb der Tag. Der Wald war zauberhaft"

Schon starb der Tag. Der Wald war zauberhaft,
und unter Farren bluteten Zyklamen,
die hohen Tannen glühten, Schaft bei Schaft,
es war ein Wind, – und schwere Düfte kamen.
Du warst von unserm weiten Weg erschlafft,
ich sagte leise deinen süßen Namen:
Da bohrte sich mit wonnewilder Kraft
aus deines Herzens weißem Liliensamen
die Feuerlilie der Leidenschaft.

Rot war der Abend – und dein Mund so rot,
wie meine Lippen sehnsuchtheiß ihn fanden,
und jene Flamme, die uns jäh durchloht,
sie leckte an den neidischen Gewanden . . .
Der Wald war stille, und der Tag war tot.
Uns aber war der Heiland auferstanden,
und mit dem Tage starben Neid und Not.
Der Mond kam groß an unsern Hügeln landen,
und leise stieg das Glück aus weißem Boot.

1. The November Day

Cold autumn is able to gag the day;
its thousand jubilant voices are still;
high from the cathedral tower there is even a strange whimper
of passing bells in November mists.

On the damp roofs there lies drowsily
white vaporous light; and with cold hands
the storm plays on the fireplace walls
the concluding octaves of a funeral chant.

2. "The day's already dead. The forest was magical"

The day's already dead. The forest was magical,
and amid the ferns cyclamens bled,
the tall firs glowed, bole by bole,
there was a wind—and heavy aromas came.
You were exhausted from our long walk,
I softly spoke your sweet name:
Then with rapturously impetuous strength
the orange-lily of passion
bored its way out of your heart's white lily-seed.

The evening was red—and your mouth so red,
when my lips, hot with longing, found it,
and that flame which blazes through us abruptly
licked our envious clothing . . .
the forest was calm, and the day was dead.
But for us the Savior had been resurrected,
and with the day envy and distress died.
A large moon came to land on our hills,
and softly happiness stepped out of its white boat.

3. "An manchem Tag ist meine Seele still"

An manchem Tag ist meine Seele still:
Ein Gotteshaus, draus alle Beter gingen.
Ein Engel nur wehrt mit den goldnen Schwingen
dem Weihrauch, der mit seinen leisen Ringen
den Jubel seiner Arme fesseln will.

Verträumte Heiligenbilder dunkeln drin
in ratlos-sehnendem Erhörenwollen:
Sie warten auf den Sonntag mit den vollen
Gestühlen und dem großen Orgelrollen—
und blasse Ampeln schwanken her und hin.

4. "Du mußt das Leben nicht verstehen"

Du mußt das Leben nicht verstehen,
dann wird es werden wie ein Fest.
Und laß dir jeden Tag geschehen
so wie ein Kind im Weitergehen
von jedem Wehen
sich viele Blüten schenken läßt.

Sie aufzusammeln und zu sparen,
das kommt dem Kind nicht in den Sinn.
Es löst sie leise aus den Haaren,
drin sie so gern gefangen waren,
und hält den lieben jungen Jahren
nach neuen seine Hände hin.

5. "Ich ließ meinen Engel lange nicht los"

Ich ließ meinen Engel lange nicht los,
und er verarmte mir in den Armen
und wurde klein, und ich wurde groß:
und auf einmal war ich das Erbarmen,
und er eine zitternde Bitte bloß.

Da hab ich ihm seine Himmel gegeben,—
und er ließ mir das Nahe, daraus er entschwand;
er lernte das Schweben, ich lernte das Leben,
und wir haben langsam einander erkannt . . .

3. "On many days my soul is calm"

On many days my soul is calm:
a house of prayer which the congregation has left.
Only an angel fends off with his golden pinions
the incense that with its gentle rings
tries to imprison his arms' rejoicing.

In it are dark, dreamy images of saints
helplessly, yearningly desirous of granting prayers:
They are waiting for Sunday with its filled
pews and the great rumbling of the organ—
and pale lamps waver back and forth.

4. "You need not understand life"

You need not understand life—
then it will become like a holiday.
And let every day come over you
just as a child going his way
lets himself be given many blossoms
by every gust of wind.

To gather them up and save them
never enters the child's mind.
He gently picks them out of his hair,
in which they were so gladly caught,
and holds out his hands to the dear
young years for new ones.

5. "For a long time I didn't let go of my angel"

For a long time I didn't let go of my angel,
and he grew impoverished in my arms,
and became small while I became big:
and all at once I was mercy,
and he merely a trembling plea.

Then I gave him his heavens—
and he left me the space around me, from which he had vanished;
he learned how to soar. I learned how to live.
and we slowly recognized each other. . . .

6. "Das ist dort, wo die letzten Hütten sind"

Das ist dort, wo die letzten Hütten sind
und neue Häuser, die mit engen Brüsten
sich drängen aus den bangen Baugerüsten
und wissen wollen, wo das Feld beginnt.

Dort bleibt der Frühling immer halb und blaß,
der Sommer fiebert hinter diesen Planken;
die Kirschenbäume und die Kinder kranken,
und nur der Herbst hat dorten irgendwas

Versöhnliches und Fernes; manchesmal
sind seine Abende von sanftem Schmelze:
die Schafe schummern, und der Hirt im Pelze
lehnt dunkel an dem letzten Lampenpfahl.

7. "Ich fürchte mich so vor der Menschen Wort"

Ich fürchte mich so vor der Menschen Wort.
Sie sprechen alles so deutlich aus:
Und dieses heißt Hund und jenes heißt Haus,
und hier ist Beginn und das Ende ist dort.

Mich bangt auch ihr Sinn, ihr Spiel mit dem Spott,
sie wissen alles, was wird und war;
kein Berg ist ihnen mehr wunderbar;
ihr Garten und Gut grenzt grade an Gott.

Ich will immer warnen und wehren: Bleibt fern.
Die Dinge singen hör ich so gern.
Ihr rührt sie an: sie sind starr und stumm.
Ihr bringt mir alle die Dinge um.

8. "Die Nacht wächst wie eine schwarze Stadt"

Die Nacht wächst wie eine schwarze Stadt,
wo nach stummen Gesetzen
sich die Gassen mit Gassen vernetzen
und sich Plätze fügen zu Plätzen,
und die bald an die tausend Türme hat.

6. "It's there, where the last construction sheds are"

It's there, where the last construction sheds are
and new houses, which with narrow breasts
push their way out of the timid scaffoldings
and want to know where the open field begins.

There springtime always remains incomplete and pallid;
summer is feverishly hot behind these boards;
the cherry trees and the children are sick,
and only autumn there has something

conciliatory and distant; sometimes
its evenings have a soft glow:
the sheep doze, and the shepherd in his fleece
leans darkly against the last lamppost.

7. "I'm so afraid of people's words"

I'm so afraid of people's words.
They pronounce everything so distinctly:
And this is called "dog" and that's called "house,"
and the beginning is here and the end is there.

I also fear their meaning, their toying with mockery;
they know everything that will be or has been;
no mountain is any longer wondrous to them;
their garden and property abut directly on God.

I always try to warn and ward off: "Stay far away!"
I so like to hear all things singing.
You people touch them, and they're stiff and mute.
You people kill all the things for me.

8. "The night grows like a black city"

The night grows like a black city
in which, in accordance with unspoken laws,
the streets entangle with streets
and squares are joined to squares,
so that it soon has some thousand towers.

Aber die Häuser der schwarzen Stadt,—
du weißt nicht, wer darin siedelt.

In ihrer Gärten schweigendem Glanz
reihen sich reigende Träume zum Tanz,—
und du weiß nicht, wer ihnen fiedelt . . .

9. "Fürchte dich nicht, sind die Astern auch alt"

Fürchte dich nicht, sind die Astern auch alt,
streut der Sturm auch den welkenden Wald
in den Gleichmut des Sees,—
die Schönheit wächst aus der engen Gestalt;
sie wurde reif, und mit milder Gewalt
zerbricht sie das alte Gefäß.

Sie kommt aus den Bäumen
in mich und in dich,
nicht um zu ruhn;
der Sommer ward ihr zu feierlich.
Aus vollen Früchten flüchtet sie sich
und steigt aus betäubenden Träumen
arm ins tägliche Tun.

10. "Du darfst nicht warten, bis Gott zu dir geht"

Du darfst nicht warten, bis Gott zu dir geht
und sagt: Ich bin.
    Ein Gott, der seine Stärke eingesteht,
hat keinen Sinn.
    Da mußt du wissen daß dich Gott durchweht
seit Anbeginn,
    und wenn dein Herz dir glüht und nichts verrät,
dann schafft er drin.

11. "Da neigt sich die Stunde und rührt mich an"

Da neigt sich die Stunde und rührt mich an
mit klarem, metallenem Schlag:

But the houses of the black city—
you don't know who has settled in them.

In the silent shining of their gardens
dreams form circles for a round dance—
and you don't know who's playing the fiddle for them. . . .

9. "Have no fear, even if the asters are old"

Have no fear, even if the asters are old,
even if the storm strews the fading woods
into the lake's equanimity—
beauty grows out of the narrow form;
it has matured, and with gentle force
it shatters the old vessel.

It comes out of the trees
and enters me and you,
but not to repose:
the summer has become too ceremonious for it.
It flees from the full fruits
and ascends from numbing dreams,
poor, into our everyday activity.

10. "You mustn't wait till God comes to you"

You mustn't wait till God comes to you
and says, "I am."
    A God who confesses his strength
makes no sense.
    Then you must know that God has pervaded you
from the very beginning,
    and whenever your heart glows and reveals nothing
he is at work within it.

11. "Now the hour inclines and touches me"

Now the hour inclines and touches me
with a clear, metallic stroke:

mir zittern die Sinne. Ich fühle: ich kann—
und ich fasse den plastischen Tag.

Nichts war noch vollendet, eh ich es erschaut,
ein jedes Werden stand still.
Meine Blicke sind reif, und wie eine Braut
kommt jedem das Ding, das er will.   ·

Nichts ist mir zu klein und ich lieb es trotzdem
und mal es auf Goldgrund und groß,
und halte es hoch, und ich weiß nicht wem
löst es die Seele los . . .

12. "Ich lebe mein Leben in wachsenden Ringen"

Ich lebe mein Leben in wachsenden Ringen,
die sich über die Dinge ziehn.
Ich werde den letzten vielleicht nicht vollbringen,
aber versuchen will ich ihn.

Ich kreise um Gott, um den uralten Turm,
und ich kreise jahrtausendelang ;
und ich weiß noch nicht: bin ich ein Falke, ein Sturm
oder ein großer Gesang.

13. "Du, Nachbar Gott, wenn ich dich manchesmal"

Du, Nachbar Gott, wenn ich dich manchesmal
in langer Nacht mit hartem Klopfen störe,—
so ists, weil ich dich selten atmen höre
und weiß: Du bist allein im Saal.
Und wenn du etwas brauchst, ist keiner da,
um deinem Tasten einen Trank zu reichen:
Ich horche immer. Gieb ein kleines Zeichen.
Ich bin ganz nah.

Nur eine schmale Wand ist zwischen uns,
durch Zufall; denn es könnte sein:
ein Rufen deines oder meines Munds—
und sie bricht ein
ganz ohne Lärm und Laut.

my senses tremble. I feel, "I can!"—
and I grasp the malleable day.

Nothing was yet completed before I viewed it,
all becoming was at a standstill.
My eyes have matured, and like a bride
the thing each man wants comes to him.

Nothing's too small for me and I love each thing anyway,
and I paint it large on a gilt ground,
and I hold it up high, and someone, I know not who,
finds his soul released by it. . . .

12. "I live my life within growing rings"

I live my life within growing rings
that spread over all the things.
Perhaps I won't complete the last ring,
but I'll try to.

I revolve around God, around the primeval tower,
and I circle for millennia;
and I still don't know whether I'm a falcon, a storm,
or a great canto.

13. "You, neighbor God, if I sometimes"

You, neighbor God, if I sometimes
disturb you with loud knocking in the long night—
it's because I rarely hear you breathing
and I know you're alone in the room.
And if you need anything, no one is there
to hold out a drink to your groping hand:
I'm always alert. Give me a small sign.
I'm very close.

There's only a thin wall between us,
by chance: because it may occur
that at a call from your lips or mine
it will break down
with no noise or sound at all.

Aus deinen Bildern ist sie aufgebaut.

Und deine Bilder stehn vor dir wie Namen.
Und wenn einmal das Licht in mir entbrennt,
mit welchem meine Tiefe dich erkennt,
vergeudet sichs als Glanz auf ihren Rahmen.

Und meine Sinne, welche schnell erlahmen,
sind ohne Heimat und von dir getrennt.

14. "Ich lebe grad, da das Jahrhundert geht"

Ich lebe grad, da das Jahrhundert geht.
Man fühlt den Wind von einem großen Blatt,
das Gott und du und ich beschrieben hat
und das sich hoch in fremden Händen dreht.

Man fühlt den Glanz von einer neuen Seite,
auf der noch Alles werden kann.

Die stillen Kräfte prüfen ihre Breite
und sehn einander dunkel an.

15. "Ich bin auf der Welt zu allein ..."

Ich bin auf der Welt zu allein und doch nicht allein genug,
um jede Stunde zu weihn.
Ich bin auf der Welt zu gering und doch nicht klein genug,
um vor dir zu sein wie ein Ding,
dunkel und klug.
Ich will meinen Willen und will meinen Willen begleiten
die Wege zur Tat;
und will in stillen, irgendwie zögernden Zeiten,
wenn etwas naht,
unter den Wissenden sein
oder allein.

Ich will dich immer spiegeln in ganzer Gestalt,
und will niemals blind sein oder zu alt
um dein schweres schwankendes Bild zu halten.
Ich will mich entfalten.

It's constructed out of images of you.

And your images stand before you like names.
And if at some time that light is kindled in me
by which my deeps recognize you,
it will be squandered as a glow on their frames.

And my senses, which quickly grow paralyzed,
are homeless and severed from you.

14. "My life coincides exactly with the close of the century"

My life coincides exactly with the close of the century.
We feel the wind of a great page
which God and you and I have written on,
and which, high up, is turning in unknown hands.

We feel the shining of a new page
on which everything may still come to be.

The silent forces are testing their extent
and gazing darkly at one another.

15. "I'm too alone in the world . . ."

I'm too alone in the world but not sufficiently alone
to consecrate every hour.
I'm too trivial in the world but not sufficiently small
to stand before you like a thing,
obscure and clever.
I want my will, and I want to accompany my will
on the way to action;
and I want, in calm, somehow hesitant times,
if something approaches,
to be among those who know,
or else alone.

I want to mirror you always in your full form,
and I never want to be blind or too old
to hold your heavy, wavering image.
I want to unfold myself.

Nirgends will ich gebogen bleiben,
denn dort bin ich gelogen, wo ich gebogen bin.
Und ich will meinen Sinn
wahr vor dir. Ich will mich beschreiben
wie ein Bild das ich sah,
lange und nah,
wie ein Wort, das ich begriff,
wie meinen täglichen Krug,
wie meiner Mutter Gesicht,
wie ein Schiff,
das mich trug
durch den tödlichsten Sturm.

16. "Wenn ich gewachsen wäre irgendwo"

Wenn ich gewachsen wäre irgendwo,
wo leichtere Tage sind und schlanke Stunden,
ich hätte dir ein großes Fest erfunden,
und meine Hände hielten dich nicht so,
wie sie dich manchmal halten, bang und hart.

Dort hätte ich gewagt, dich zu vergeuden,
du grenzenlose Gegenwart.
Wie einen Ball
hätt ich dich in alle wogenden Freuden
hineingeschleudert, daß einer dich finge
und deinem Fall
mit hohen Händen entgegenspringe,
du Ding der Dinge.

Ich hätte dich wie eine Klinge
blitzen lassen.
Vom goldensten Ringe
ließ ich dein Feuer umfassen,
und er müßte mirs halten
über die weißeste Hand.

Gemalt hätt ich dich: nicht an die Wand,
an den Himmel selber von Rand zu Rand,
und hätt dich gebildet, wie ein Gigant
dich bilden würde: als Berg, als Brand,
als Samum, wachsend aus Wüstensand—

I don't want to remain bent anywhere,
because where I am bent I am falsified.
And I want my mind
to be true in your presence. I want to describe myself
like an image I have seen,
lengthily and closely,
like a word I have understood,
like my everyday pitcher,
like my mother's face,
like a ship
that has borne me
through the deadliest storm.

16. "If I had grown in some place"

If I had grown in some place
where the days are less heavy and the hours are slender,
I would have invented a great festival for you,
and my hands wouldn't hold you
as they sometimes hold you, timorously and convulsively.

There I would have ventured to squander you,
you limitless present time.
Like a ball
I'd have hurled you into every surging
joy, for someone to catch you
and leap to meet
your falling with upraised hands,
you thing of things.

I'd have let you gleam forth
like a sword blade.
I'd have let your fire be enclosed
in the most golden of rings,
which would have had to hold it for me
above the whitest of hands.

I'd have painted you: not on the wall,
but from one edge to the other of the sky itself,
and I'd have pictured you the way a giant
would have pictured you: as a mountain, as a conflagration,
as a simoon growing out of desert sand—

oder
es kann auch sein: ich fand
dich einmal. . .

        Meine Freunde sind weit,
ich höre kaum noch ihr Lachen schallen;
und du: du bist aus dem Nest gefallen,
bist ein junger Vogel mit gelben Krallen
und großen Augen und tust mir leid.
(Meine Hand ist dir viel zu breit.)
Und ich heb mit dem Finger vom Quell einen Tropfen
und lausche, ob du ihn lechzend langst,
und ich fühle dein Herz und meines klopfen
und beide aus Angst.

17. "Was wirst du tun, Gott, wenn ich sterbe?"

Was wirst du tun, Gott, wenn ich sterbe?
Ich bin dein Krug (wenn ich zerscherbe?)
Ich bin dein Trank (wenn ich verderbe?)
Bin dein Gewand und dein Gewerbe,
mit mir verlierst du deinen Sinn.

Nach mir hast du kein Haus, darin
dich Worte, nah und warm, begrüßen.
Es fällt von deinen müden Füßen
die Samtsandale, die ich bin.

Dein großer Mantel läßt dich los.
Dein Blick, den ich mit meiner Wange
warm, wie mit einem Pfühl, empfange,
wird kommen, wird mich suchen, lange—
und legt beim Sonnenuntergange
sich fremden Steinen in den Schooß.

Was wirst du tun, Gott? Ich bin bange.

18. "Ich komme aus meinen Schwingen heim"

Ich komme aus meinen Schwingen heim,
mit denen ich mich verlor.

or
it may also be: I found
you once . . .

          My friends are far away,
I can scarcely still hear their laughter resounding;
and you: you have fallen from the nest,
you're a young bird with yellow claws
and big eyes, and I'm sorry for you.
(My hand is much too wide for you.)
And with my finger I lift a drop from the spring
and listen to hear whether you reach it in your thirst,
and I feel your heart and mine beating,
both of them from anxiety.

17. "What will you do, God, if I die?"

What will you do, God, if I die?
I am your pitcher (if I shatter?)
I am your drink (if I spoil?)
I am your garment and your occupation;
losing me, you lose your meaning.

With me gone, you have no house in which
words, close and warm, will greet you.
From your weary feet falls
the velvet sandal that I am.

Your great mantle drops from you.
Your gaze, which with my cheek I
receive warmly, as if with a pillow,
will come, will seek me, for a long time—
and at sunset will lie down
in the lap of unfamiliar stones.

What will you do, God? I'm afraid.

18. "I return home from my pinioned flight"

I return home from my pinioned flight,
on which I went astray.

Ich war Gesang, und Gott, der Reim,
rauscht noch in meinem Ohr.

Ich werde wieder still und schlicht,
und meine Stimme steht;
es senkte sich mein Angesicht
zu besserem Gebet.
Den andern war ich wie ein Wind,
da ich sie rüttelnd rief.
Weit war ich, wo die Engel sind,
hoch, wo das Licht in Nichts zerrinnt—
Gott aber dunkelt tief.

Die Engel sind das letzte Wehn
an seines Wipfels Saum;
daß sie aus seinen Ästen gehn,
ist ihnen wie ein Traum.
Sie glauben dort dem Lichte mehr
als Gottes schwarzer Kraft,
es flüchtete sich Lucifer
in ihre Nachbarschaft.

Er ist der Fürst im Land des Lichts,
und seine Stirne steht
so steil am großen Glanz des Nichts,
daß er, versengten Angesichts,
nach Finsternissen fleht.
Er ist der helle Gott der Zeit,
zu dem sie laut erwacht,
und weil er oft in Schmerzen schreit
und oft in Schmerzen lacht,
glaubt sie an seine Seligkeit
und hangt an seiner Macht.

Die Zeit ist wie ein welker Rand
an einem Buchenblatt.
Sie ist das glänzende Gewand,
das Gott verworfen hat,
als Er, der immer Tiefe war,
ermüdete des Flugs
und sich verbarg vor jedem Jahr,
bis ihm sein wurzelhaftes Haar
durch alle Dinge wuchs.

I was song, and God the rhyme
still rumbles in my ear.

Again I become calm and simple,
and my voice is still;
my face is lowered
for a better prayer.
To the others I was like a wind,
rousing them as I called to them.
I was far off, where the angels dwell,
high up, where the light dissolves into nothingness—
but God is profoundly dark.

The angels are the final breeze
stirring the edge of his treetop;
that they depart from his boughs
is like a dream to them.
There they believe in the light more
than they do in God's black strength;
Lucifer fled for refuge
into their vicinity.

He is the prince in the land of light,
and his brow stands
so steeply against the mighty glow of the nothingness
that, with a singed face, he
begs for periods of darkness.
He is the bright god of time,
for whom it loudly awakes,
and because he often cries out in his pain
and often laughs in his pain;
it believes he is blissful
and relies on his power.

Time is like the faded rim
of a beech leaf.
It is the shining garment
that God rejected
when he, who was always profundity,
grew weary of flying
and hid himself from every year
until his rootlike hair
grew through all things.

19. "Ich bete wieder, du Erlauchter"

Ich bete wieder, du Erlauchter,
du hörst mich wieder durch den Wind,
weil meine Tiefen niegebrauchter
rauschender Worte mächtig sind.

Ich war zerstreut; an Widersacher
in Stücken war verteilt mein Ich.
O Gott, mich lachten alle Lacher
und alle Trinker tranken mich.

In Höfen hab ich mich gesammelt
aus Abfall und aus altem Glas,
mit halbem Mund dich angestammelt,
dich, Ewiger aus Ebenmaß.
Wie hob ich meine halben Hände
zu dir in namenlosem Flehn,
daß ich die Augen wiederfände,
mit denen ich dich angesehn.

Ich war ein Haus nach einem Brand,
darin nur Mörder manchmal schlafen,
eh ihre hungerigen Strafen
sie weiterjagen in das Land;
ich war wie eine Stadt am Meer,
wenn eine Seuche sie bedrängte,
die sich wie eine Leiche schwer
den Kindern an die Hände hängte.

Ich war mir fremd wie irgendwer,
und wußte nur von ihm, daß er
einst meine junge Mutter kränkte
als sie mich trug,
und daß ihr Herz, das eingeengte,
sehr schmerzhaft an mein Keimen schlug.

Jetzt bin ich wieder aufgebaut
aus allen Stücken meiner Schande,
und sehne mich nach einem Bande,
nach einem einigen Verstande,
der mich wie *ein* Ding überschaut,—
nach deines Herzens großen Händen—

19. "I pray once more, illustrious one"

I pray once more, illustrious one,
once more you hear me through the wind,
because my deeps are capable
of never-used, thunderous words.

I was scattered; clashes with adversaries
had broken my self into small pieces.
O God, I was the laugh of every laugher
and the beverage of every bibber.

I gathered myself together in courtyards
out of refuse and old glass:
with half a mouth I stammered to you,
to you, eternal lord of symmetry.
How I raised my half hands
to you in nameless beseeching,
so that I might regain the eyes
with which I had beheld you!

I was a house after a fire,
in which only murderers sometimes sleep
before their hungry punishment
chases them farther afield;
I was like a city by the sea
when a plague has oppressed it,
attaching itself to children's hands
as heavily as a corpse.

I was as much a stranger to myself as anyone,
and of him I knew only that he
once troubled my young mother
when she carried me,
and that her tightened heart
beat very painfully against my fetal form.

Now I am reconstructed
out of all the pieces of my disgrace,
and I yearn for a bonding,
for a unified understanding
that will survey me as one single thing—
I yearn for your heart's big hands

(o kämen sie doch auf mich zu).
Ich zähle mich, mein Gott, und du,
du hast das Recht, mich zu verschwenden.

20. "Ich bin derselbe noch, der kniete"

Ich bin derselbe noch, der kniete
vor dir in mönchischem Gewand:
der tiefe, dienende Levite,
den du erfüllt, der dich erfand.
Die Stimme einer stillen Zelle,
an der die Welt vorüberweht,—
und du bist immer noch die Welle
die über alle Dinge geht.

Es *ist* nichts andres. Nur ein Meer,
aus dem die Länder manchmal steigen.
Es *ist* nichts andres denn ein Schweigen
von schönen Engeln und von Geigen,
und der Verschwiegene ist der,
zu dem sich alle Dinge neigen,
von seiner Stärke Strahlen schwer.

Bist du denn Alles, – ich der Eine,
der sich ergiebt und sich empört?
Bin ich denn nicht das Allgemeine,
bin ich nicht *Alles*, wenn ich weine,
und du der Eine, der es hört?

Hörst du denn etwas neben mir?
Sind da noch Stimmen außer meiner?
Ist da ein Sturm? Auch ich bin einer,
und meine Wälder winken dir.

Ist da ein Lied, ein krankes, kleines,
das dich am Micherhören stört,—
auch ich bin eines, höre meines,
das einsam ist und unerhört.

Ich bin derselbe noch, der bange
dich manchmal fragte, wer du seist.
Nach jedem Sonnenuntergange

(oh, if they'd only come to me!).
I am counting myself up, God, and you,
you have the right to spend me.

20. "I'm still the same man who knelt"

I'm still the same man who knelt
before you in a monk's habit:
the lowly acolyte who serves you,
the man you filled, the man who invented you.
The voice of a quiet cell
past which the world wafts—
and you are still always the wave
that washes over all things.

Nothing else exists. Only a sea
from which land sometimes emerges.
Nothing else exists but a silence
of lovely angels and of violins,
and the discreetly silent one is he
to whom all things bow down,
heavy with the rays of his strength.

Are you then everything, and I the only one
who surrenders himself and who rebels?
Am I not, then, the generality,
am I not *everything* when I weep,
and you the only one who hears it?

Do you, then, hear anything besides me?
Do voices still exist other than mine?
Is a storm there? I am one, too,
and my forests beckon to you.

If a song is there, a small, sickly one
which hinders you from granting my wishes—
I'm one, too, listen to mine,
which is solitary and unusual.

I'm still the same man who in fear
sometimes asked you who you are.
After every sunset

bin ich verwundet und verwaist,
ein blasser Allem Abgelöster
und ein Verschmähter jeder Schar,
und alle Dinge stehn wie Klöster,
in denen ich gefangen war.
Dann brauch ich dich, du Eingeweihter,
du sanfter Nachbar jeder Not,
du meines Leidens leiser Zweiter,
du Gott, dann brauch ich dich wie Brot.
Du weißt vielleicht nicht, wie die Nächte
für Menschen, die nicht schlafen, sind:
da sind sie alle Ungerechte,
der Greis, die Jungfrau und das Kind.
Sie fahren auf wie totgesagt,
von schwarzen Dingen nah umgeben,
und ihre weißen Hände beben,
verwoben in ein wildes Leben
wie Hunde in ein Bild der Jagd.
Vergangenes steht noch bevor,
und in der Zukunft liegen Leichen,
ein Mann im Mantel pocht am Tor,
und mit dem Auge und dem Ohr
ist noch kein erstes Morgenzeichen,
kein Hahnruf ist noch zu erreichen.
Die Nacht ist wie ein großes Haus.
Und mit der Angst der wunden Hände
reißen sie Türen in die Wände,—
dann kommen Gänge ohne Ende,
und nirgends ist ein Tor hinaus.

Und so, mein Gott, ist *jede* Nacht;
immer sind welche aufgewacht,
die gehn und gehn und dich nicht finden.
Hörst du sie mit dem Schritt von Blinden
das Dunkel treten?
Auf Treppen, die sich niederwinden,
hörst du sie beten?
Hörst du sie fallen auf den schwarzen Steinen?
Du mußt sie weinen hören; denn sie weinen.

Ich suche dich, weil sie vorübergehn
an meiner Tür. Ich kann sie beinah sehn.

I am wounded and orphaned,
a pale man detached from everything
and a man scorned by every group,
and all things are like cloisters
in which I was imprisoned.
Then I need you, consecrated one,
you gentle neighbor to every distress,
you quiet second to my sorrow,
you God, then I need you like bread.
Perhaps you don't know what nights
are like for people who can't sleep:
then they're all unrighteous,
the old man, the virgin, and the child.
They start up as if their death were imminent,
tightly surrounded by black things,
and their white hands tremble,
woven into a wild existence
like dogs into a tapestry of the hunt.
Their past still stands ahead of them,
and in the future lie corpses;
a cloaked man knocks at the gate,
and for eye and ear
there is still no first sign of morning,
no cockcrow is attainable yet.
The night is like a large house.
And in the anxiety of their bleeding hands
they tear doors out of the walls—
then come endless corridors,
and nowhere is there a gate leading out.

And, my God, *every* night is like that;
there are always some people awakened
who walk and walk but can't find you.
Do you hear them treading the darkness
with blind men's steps?
On staircases that wind downwards
do you hear them praying?
Do you hear them falling on the black stones?
You must hear them weeping, for they weep.

I seek you because they are passing
by my door. I can almost see them.

Wen soll ich rufen, wenn nicht *den,*
der dunkel ist und nächtiger als Nacht.
Den Einzigen, der ohne Lampe wacht
und doch nicht bangt; den Tiefen, den das Licht
noch nicht verwöhnt hat und von dem ich weiß,
weil er mit Bäumen aus der Erde bricht
und weil er leis
als Duft in mein gesenktes Angesicht
aus Erde steigt.

21. "Alle, welche dich suchen, versuchen dich"

Alle, welche dich suchen, versuchen dich.
Und die, so dich finden, binden dich
an Bild und Gebärde.

Ich aber will dich begreifen
wie dich die Erde begreift;
mit meinem Reifen
reift
dein Reich.

Ich will von dir keine Eitelkeit,
die dich beweist.
Ich weiß, daß die Zeit
anders heißt
als du.

Tu mir kein Wunder zulieb.
Gieb deinen Gesetzen recht,
die von Geschlecht zu Geschlecht
sichtbarer sind.

22. "Weißt du von jenen Heiligen, mein Herr?"

Weißt du von jenen Heiligen, mein Herr?

Sie fühlten auch verschloßne Klosterstuben

Whom shall I call, if not *that one*
who is dark and more nocturnal than the night?
That only one who is awake without a lamp
and yet is unafraid; that profound one, whom the light
has not yet pampered, and whom I know about
because with trees he breaks out of the earth
and because he quietly
rises from the ground like a vapor
onto my lowered face.

21. "All those who seek you try you"

All those who seek you try[1] you.
And those who find you bind you
to image and gesture.

But I want to understand you
the way that the earth understands you;
with my ripening,
so ripens
your kingdom.

I want no vanity from you
which proves your existence.
I know that time
has a name different
from yours.

Perform no miracle on my account.
Let your normal laws operate,
which from generation to generation
become more and more visible.

22. "Do you know about those holy men, my Lord?"

Do you know about those holy men, my Lord?

They felt that even closed monastic cells

---

[1] In every sense of "try." The verb *versuchen* can mean "attempt," "taste of," and "tempt." No doubt the ambiguity was intentional on Rilke's part.

zu nahe an Gelächter und Geplärr,
so daß sie tief sich in die Erde gruben.

Ein jeder atmete mit seinem Licht
die kleine Luft in seiner Grube aus,
vergaß sein Alter und sein Angesicht
und lebte wie ein fensterloses Haus
und starb nichtmehr, als wär er lange tot.

Sie lasen selten; alles war verdorrt,
als wäre Frost in jedes Buch gekrochen,
und wie die Kutte hing von ihren Knochen,
so hing der Sinn herab von jedem Wort.
Sie redeten einander nichtmehr an,
wenn sie sich fühlten in den schwarzen Gängen,
sie ließen ihre langen Haare hängen,
und keiner wußte, ob sein Nachbarmann
nicht stehend starb.

                    In einem runden Raum,
wo Silberlampen sich von Balsam nährten,
versammelten sich manchmal die Gefährten
vor goldnen Türen wie vor goldnen Gärten
und schauten voller Mißtraun in den Traum
und rauschten leise mit den langen Bärten.

Ihr Leben war wie tausend Jahre groß,
seit es sich nichtmehr schied in Nacht und Helle;
sie waren, wie gewälzt von einer Welle,
zurückgekehrt in ihrer Mutter Schooß.
Sie saßen rundgekrümmt wie Embryos
mit großen Köpfen und mit kleinen Händen
und aßen nicht, als ob sie Nahrung fänden
aus jener Erde, die sie schwarz umschloß.

Jetzt zeigt man sie den tausend Pilgern, die
aus Stadt und Steppe zu dem Kloster wallen.
Seit dreimal hundert Jahren liegen sie,
und ihre Leiber können nicht zerfallen.
Das Dunkel häuft sich wie ein Licht das rußt
auf ihren langen lagernden Gestalten,
die unter Tüchern heimlich sich erhalten,—
und ihrer Hände ungelöstes Falten
liegt ihnen wie Gebirge auf der Brust.

were too near to laughter and chatter,
so that they dug themselves deep into the ground.

Each one of them, along with his candle,
breathed out the little air in his pit,
forgetting his age and his face,
and lived like a windowless house
and died no longer, as if already long dead.

They seldom read; everything was withered
as if frost had crept into every book,
and just as their habits hung down from their bones,
the sense of every word hung down from it.
They no longer addressed one another
when they sensed the other's presence in the black corridors;
they let their long hair hang down,
and none of them knew whether his neighbor
hadn't died on his feet.

                    In a circular room
where silver lamps were fed on balsam,
the companions sometimes assembled
before golden doors, as if before golden gardens,
and gazed, full of mistrust, into their dream
and rustled softly with their long beards.

Their life was as large as a thousand years,
ever since it was no longer divided between night and brightness;
as if rolled away by a wave, they had
returned to their mothers' wombs.
They sat curled up like embryos
with big heads and small hands,
and didn't eat, as if they found nourishment
in that earth which blackly enclosed them.

Now they are shown to the thousand pilgrims who
wander to the monastery from city and steppe.
For thrice a hundred years they have been lying there,
and their bodies cannot crumble.
Darkness is heaped up like a smoky candle
on their long, recumbent forms,
which are mysteriously preserved beneath cloths—
and their hands, never unfolded,
lie on their breasts like mountains.

Du großer alter Herzog des Erhabnen:
hast du vergessen, diesen Eingegrabnen
den Tod zu schicken, der sie ganz verbraucht,
weil sie sich tief in Erde eingetaucht?
Sind die, die sich Verstorbenen vergleichen,
am ähnlichsten der Unvergänglichkeit?
1st das das große Leben deiner Leichen,
das überdauern sol den Tod der Zeit?

Sind sie dir noch zu deinen Plänen gut?
Erhältst du unvergängliche Gefäße,
die du, der allen Maßen Ungemäße,
einmal erfüllen willst mit deinem Blut?

23. "Ein Pilgermorgen. Von den harten Lagern"

Ein Pilgermorgen. Von den harten Lagern,
auf das ein jeder wie vergiftet fiel,
erhebt sich bei dem ersten Glockenspiel
ein Volk von hagern Morgensegen-Sagern,
auf das die frühe Sonne niederbrennt:

Bärtige Männer, welche sich verneigen,
Kinder, die ernsthaft aus den Pelzen steigen,
und in den Mänteln, schwer von ihrem Schweigen,
die braunen Fraun von Tiflis und Taschkent.
Christen mit den Gebärden des Islam
sind um die Brunnen, halten ihre Hände
wie flache Schalen hin, wie Gegenstände,
in die die Flut wie eine Seele kam.

Sie neigen das Gesicht hinein und trinken,
reißen die Kleider auf mit ihrer Linken
und halten sich das Wasser an die Brust
als wärs ein kühles weinendes Gesicht,
das von den Schmerzen auf der Erde spricht.

Und diese Schmerzen stehen rings umher
mit welken Augen; und du weißt nicht wer
sie sind und waren. Knechte oder Bauern,
vielleicht Kaufleute, welche Wohlstand sahn,
vielleicht auch laue Mönche, die nicht dauern,

You great old duke of the sublime:
have you forgotten to send these buried men
death which will completely consume them,
because they immersed themselves deep in the earth?
Are those who compare themselves to the dead
those most similar to immortality?
Is this the great life of your corpses
which is to outlast the death of time?

Are they still suitable for your plans?
Are you preserving imperishable vessels
which you, unproportioned to all measure,
will some day fill with your blood?

23. "A pilgrims' morning. From the hard pallets"

A pilgrims' morning. From the hard pallets
onto which each one had fallen as if poisoned
there arises at the first peal of bells
a people of scrawny morning-blessing reciters,
onto whom the early sun burns down:

Bearded men who bow,
children who solemnly climb out of their fur bedding,
and in their capes, heavy with their silence,
the brown women from Tiflis and Tashkent.
Christians with the gestures of Islam
are around the wells, holding their hands
out like shallow bowls, like objects
into which the water has flowed like a soul.

They lower their faces into it and drink,
tear their clothing open with their left hand,
and hold the water to their breast
as if it were a cool, weeping face
speaking of earthly sorrows.

And these sorrows stand round about
with faded eyes; and you don't know who
they are and were. Servants or peasants,
perhaps merchants who once knew prosperity,
perhaps even lukewarm monks who don't last

und Diebe, die auf die Versuchung lauern,
offene Mädchen, die verkümmert kauern,
und Irrende in einem Wald von Wahn—:
alle wie Fürsten, die in tiefem Trauern
die Überflüsse von sich abgetan.
Wie Weise alle, welche viel erfahren,
Erwählte, welche in der Wüste waren,
wo Gott sie nährte durch ein fremdes Tier;
Einsame, die durch Ebenen gegangen
mit vielen Winden an den dunklen Wangen,
von einer Sehnsucht fürchtig und befangen
und doch so wundersam erhöht von ihr.
Gelöste aus dem Alltag, eingeschaltet
in große Orgeln und in Chorgesang,
und Knieende, wie Steigende gestaltet;
Fahnen mit Bildern, welche lang
verborgen waren und zusammgefaltet:

Jetzt hängen sie sich langsam wieder aus.

Und manche stehn und schaun nach einem Haus,
darin die Pilger, welche krank sind, wohnen;
denn eben wand sich dort ein Mönch heraus,
die Haare schlaff und die Sutane kraus,
das schattige Gesicht voll kranker Blaus
und ganz verdunkelt von Dämonen.

Er neigte sich, als bräch er sich entzwei,
und warf sich in zwei Stücken auf die Erde,
die jetzt an seinem Munde wie ein Schrei
zu hängen schien und so als sei
sie seiner Arme wachsende Gebärde.

Und langsam ging sein Fall an ihm vorbei.

Er flog empor, als ob er Flügel spürte,
und sein erleichtertes Gefühl verführte
ihn zu dem Glauben seiner Vogelwerdung.
Er hing in seinen magern Armen schmal,
wie eine schiefgeschobne Marionette,
und glaubte, daß er große Schwingen hätte
und daß die Welt schon lange wie ein Tal
sich ferne unter seinen Füßen glätte.

and thieves lurking in wait for something tempting,
prostitutes crouching in atrophy,
and madmen in a forest of delusion—
all like princes who in deep mourning
have put aside all abundance.
All like wise folk, who learn much,
chosen people who have been in the wilderness,
where God fed them by the agency of a strange animal;
lonely people who have walked across plains
with many winds on their dark cheeks,
fearful and disconcerted by a longing
and yet so marvelously uplifted by it.
Folk released from ordinary life, made to participate
in mighty organs and choral song,
and people kneeling, in the form of folk ascending;
pictured banners that had long
been stored away and rolled up:

Now they are slowly hung out again.

And many stand and gaze at a house
in which the pilgrims who are sick reside;
for just now a monk has tortuously left it,
his hair limp and his cassock crooked,
his shadowed face full of sickly blue patches
and completely darkened by demons.

He bowed as if breaking in two,
and threw himself in two pieces onto the earth,
which now seemed to hang on his lips
like a cry, and as if it were
the growing gesture of his arms.

And slowly his fall passed away from him.

He flew upward, as if he felt wings,
and his relieved feelings seduced
him into the belief he had become a bird.
He hung slenderly in his skinny arms,
like a marionette that has been pushed awry,
and he believed he had large pinions
and that for some time now the world, like a valley,
was becoming level far below his feet.

Ungläubig sah er sich mit einem Mal
herabgelassen auf die fremde Stätte
und auf den grünen Meergrund seiner Qual.
Und war ein Fisch und wand sich schlank und schwamm
durch tiefes Wasser, still und silbergrau,
sah Quallen hangen am Korallenstamm
und sah die Haare einer Meerjungfrau,
durch die das Wasser rauschte wie ein Kamm.
Und kam zu Land und war ein Bräutigam
bei einer Toten, wie man ihn erwählt
damit kein Mädchen fremd und unvermählt
des Paradieses Wiesenland beschritte.

Er folgte ihr und ordnete die Tritte
und tanzte rund, sie immer in der Mitte,
und seine Arme tanzten rund um ihn.
Dann horchte er, als wäre eine dritte
Gestalt ganz sachte in das Spiel getreten,
die diesem Tanzen nicht zu glauben schien.
Und da erkannte er: jetzt mußt du beten;
denn dieser ist es, welcher den Propheten
wie eine große Krone sich verliehn.
Wir halten ihn, um den wir täglich flehten,
wir ernten ihn, den einstens Ausgesäeten,
und kehren heim mit ruhenden Geräten
in langen Reihen wie in Melodien.
Und er verneigte sich ergriffen, tief.

Aber der Alte war, als ob er schliefe,
und sah es nicht, obwohl sein Aug nicht schlief.

Und er verneigte sich in solche Tiefe,
daß ihm ein Zittern durch die Glieder lief.
Aber der Alte ward es nicht gewahr.

Da faßte sich der kranke Mönch am Haar
und schlug sich wie ein Kleid an einen Baum.
Aber der Alte stand und sah es kaum.

Da nahm der kranke Mönch sich in die Hände
wie man ein Richtschwert in die Hände nimmt,
und hieb und hieb, verwundete die Wände
und stieß sich endlich in den Grund ergrimmt.
Aber der Alte blickte unbestimmt.

It was in disbelief that he suddenly found himself
let down on that unfamiliar place
and on the green ocean bed of his torment.
And he was a fish and twisted nimbly and swam
through deep water, silent and silvery gray,
saw jellyfish hanging on the coral stem
and saw a mermaid's hair
through which the water rustled like a comb.
And he came ashore and was a bridegroom
to a dead woman, as a man is chosen
so that no girl will tread the meadowland
of paradise as a stranger, and unwed.

He followed her and arranged the steps
and did a round dance, she always in the center,
and his arms danced around *him*.
Then he stopped to listen, as if a third
figure had joined in the sport very quietly,
one who seemed not to believe in that dancing.
And then he realized: "Now you must pray,
because this is he who lent himself
to the prophets like a great crown.
We hold the one for whom we implored daily;
we harvest him who once was sown as seed,
and we return home with tools at rest
in long files as if in melodies."
And, greatly stirred, he made a low bow.

But the Old One acted as if he were asleep,
and didn't see this, though his eyes didn't sleep.

And the monk bowed down so low
that a tremor ran through his limbs.
But the Old One was unaware of this.

Then the sick monk grasped his own hair
and beat himself against a tree like a garment.
But the Old One stood there and hardly saw it.

Then the sick monk took himself in his hands
the way one takes an executioner's sword in one's hands,
and struck and struck, wounding the walls
and finally driving himself into the ground in fury.
But the Old One looked on in an indeterminate way.

Da riß der Mönch sein Kleid sich ab wie Rinde
und knieend hielt er es dem Alten hin.

Und sieh: er kam. Kam wie zu einem Kinde
und sagte sanft: Weißt du auch *wer ich bin?*
Das wußte er. Und legte sich gelinde
dem Greis wie eine Geige unters Kinn.

24. "Jetzt reifen schon die roten Berberitzen"

Jetzt reifen schon die roten Berberitzen,
alternde Astern atmen schwach im Beet.
Wer jetzt nicht reich ist, da der Sommer geht,
wird immer warten und sich nie besitzen.

Wer jetzt nicht seine Augen schließen kann,
gewiß, daß eine Fülle von Gesichten
in ihm nur wartet bis die Nacht begann,
um sich in seinem Dunkel aufzurichten:—
der ist vergangen wie ein alter Mann.

Dem kommt nichts mehr, dem stößt kein Tag mehr zu,
und alles lügt ihn an, was ihm geschieht;
auch du, mein Gott. Und wie ein Stein bist du,
welcher ihn täglich in die Tiefe zieht.

25. "In tiefen Nächten grab ich dich, du Schatz"

In tiefen Nächten grab ich dich, du Schatz.
Denn alle Überflüsse, die ich sah,
sind Armut und armsäliger Ersatz
für deine Schönheit, die noch nie geschah.

Aber der Weg zu dir ist furchtbar weit
und, weil ihn lange keiner ging, verweht.
O du bist einsam. Du bist Einsamkeit,
du Herz, das zu entfernten Talen geht.

Und meine Hände, welche blutig sind
vom Graben, heb ich offen in den Wind,
so daß sie sich verzweigen wie ein Baum.

Then the monk tore off his habit like bark
and, kneeling, held it out to the Old One.

And behold: he came. Came as if to a child
and said softly: "Do you also know *who I am?*"
He did know. And gently he placed himself
beneath the Old One's chin like a violin.

24. "The red barberries are already ripening"

The red barberries are already ripening,
aging asters are breathing weakly in the flowerbed.
Whoever is not rich now that the summer is ending
will always wait and never possess himself.

Whoever cannot close his eyes now
in the certainty that an abundance of visions
is merely waiting within him for the night to begin,
in order to erect themselves in his darkness—
he has perished like an old man.

For him nothing more comes, for him no further day arrives,
and everything that happens to him tells him lies;
even you, my God. And you are like a stone
dragging him daily into the depths.

25. "On deep nights I dig you up, you treasure"

On deep nights I dig you up, you treasure.
For all the abundance I have seen
is poverty and a wretched substitute
for your beauty, which has never yet been known.

But the way to you is terribly long
and, because no one has followed it for so long, obliterated.
Oh, you are lonely! You are solitude,
your heart journeying to remote valleys.

And my hands, which are bloody
with digging, I lift open into the wind,
so that they branch out like a tree.

Ich sauge dich mit ihnen aus dem Raum
als hättest du dich einmal dort zerschellt
in einer ungeduldigen Gebärde,
und fielest jetzt, eine zerstäubte Welt,
aus fernen Sternen wieder auf die Erde
sanft wie ein Frühlingsregen fällt.

26. "Vielleicht, daß ich durch schwere Berge gehe"

Vielleicht, daß ich durch schwere Berge gehe
in harten Adern, wie ein Erz allein;
und bin so tief, daß ich kein Ende sehe
und keine Ferne: alles wurde Nähe
und alle Nähe wurde Stein.

Ich bin ja noch kein Wissender im Wehe,—
so macht mich dieses große Dunkel klein;
bist *Du* es aber: mach dich schwer, brich ein:
daß deine ganze Hand an mir geschehe
und ich an dir mit meinem ganzen Schrein.

27. "Denn, Herr, die großen Städte sind"

Denn, Herr, die großen Städte sind
verlorene und aufgelöste;
wie Flucht vor Flammen ist die größte,—
und ist kein Trost, daß er sie tröste,
und ihre kleine Zeit verrinnt.

Da leben Menschen, leben schlecht und schwer,
in tiefen Zimmern, bange von Gebärde,
geängsteter denn eine Erstlingsherde;
und draußen wacht und atmet deine Erde,
sie aber sind und wissen es nicht mehr.

Da wachsen Kinder auf an Fensterstufen,
die immer in demselben Schatten sind,
und wissen nicht, daß draußen Blumen rufen
zu einem Tag voll Weite, Glück und Wind,—
und müssen Kind sein und sind traurig Kind.

With them I absorb you from space
as if you had once been shattered there
in an impatient gesture,
and were now falling, a pulverized world,
back to earth from distant stars
as gently as a springtime rain falls.

26. "Perhaps I am walking through heavy mountains"

Perhaps I am walking through heavy mountains
in hard veins, alone like an ore;
and am so deep that I can see no end
and no distance: all has become nearness
and all nearness has become stone.

Indeed, I'm not yet knowledgeable about sorrow—
thus this great darkness diminishes me;
but if it's *you*: become heavy, break in:
so that your entire hand may befall me,
and I you with all my outcry.

27. "For, Lord, big cities are"

For, Lord, big cities are
lost, dissolved places;
the largest one is like an escape from flames—
and no consolation can console it,
and its brief time runs out.

In it live people, they live badly and difficultly,
in low rooms, with timorous gestures,
more anguished than a flock of firstborn sheep;
and, outside, your earth is awake and breathing,
but they exist and no longer know that they do.

There children grow up at tiers of windows
which are always in the same shadow,
and they don't know that, outdoors, flowers call them
to a day full of breadth, happiness, and breezes—
they must live a child's life but they do so sadly.

Da blühen Jungfraun auf zum Unbekannten
und sehnen sich nach ihrer Kindheit Ruh;
das aber ist nicht da, wofür sie brannten,
und zitternd schließen sie sich wieder zu.
Und haben in verhüllten Hinterzimmern
die Tage der enttäuschten Mutterschaft,
der langen Nächte willenloses Wimmern
und kalte Jahre ohne Kampf und Kraft.
Und ganz im Dunkel stehn die Sterbebetten,
und langsam sehnen sie sich dazu hin;
und sterben lange, sterben wie in Ketten
und gehen aus wie eine Bettlerin.

28. "O wo ist der, der aus Besitz und Zeit"

O wo ist der, der aus Besitz und Zeit
zu seiner großen Armut so erstarkte,
daß er die Kleider abtat auf dem Markte
und bar einherging vor des Bischofs Kleid.
Der Innigste und Liebendste von allen,
der kam und lebte wie ein junges Jahr;
der braune Bruder deiner Nachtigallen,
in dem ein Wundern und ein Wohlgefallen
und ein Entzücken an der Erde war.

Denn er war keiner von den immer Müdern,
die freudeloser werden nach und nach,
mit kleinen Blumen wie mit kleinen Brüdern
ging er den Wiesenrand entlang und sprach.
Und sprach von sich und wie er sich verwende
so daß es allem eine Freude sei;
und seines hellen Herzens war kein Ende,
und kein Geringes ging daran vorbei.

Er kam aus Licht zu immer tieferm Lichte,
und seine Zelle stand in Heiterkeit.
Das Lächeln wuchs auf seinem Angesichte
und hatte seine Kindheit und Geschichte
und wurde reif wie eine Mädchenzeit.

Und wenn er sang, so kehrte selbst das Gestern
und das Vergessene zurück und kam;

There maidens blossom out into the unknown
and long for the repose of their childhood;
but that for which they burned isn't there,
and tremblingly they shut their petals again.
And in shrouded back rooms they live
their days of disappointed motherhood,
the will-less whimpering of the long nights,
and cold years without struggle or strength.
And the deathbeds stand completely in the dark,
and slowly they yearn to lie in them;
and they're a long time dying, they die as if in chains,
and they breathe their last like beggar women.

28. "Oh, where is he who, forsaking possessions and time"

Oh, where is he who, forsaking possessions and time,
grew so strong to attain his great poverty
that he cast off his clothing in the marketplace
and walked about naked before the bishop's robes?
The most inward and loving of all,
he who came and lived like a youthful year;
the brown-clad brother of your nightingales,
in whom was an astonishment at, a delight in,
and a rapturous love for, the earth.

For he wasn't one of those who are always more tired
and who gradually become more joyless;
he'd walk along the margin of the meadow speaking
to little flowers as if to little brothers.
And he spoke of himself and how he applied himself
so that his efforts might be a joy to all;
and there was no limit to the brightness of his heart,
which left not even a trifle pass it by.

He emerged from the light into more and more profound light,
and his cell was always cheerful.
Smiles grew on his face
and had their childhood and history
and became ripe like a girlhood.

And when he sang, even yesterdays and forgotten things
turned back and came again;

und eine Stille wurde in den Nestern,
und nur die Herzen schrieen in den Schwestern,
die er berührte wie ein Bräutigam.

Dann aber lösten seines Liedes Pollen
sich leise los aus seinem roten Mund
und trieben träumend zu den Liebevollen
und fielen in die offenen Corollen
und sanken langsam auf den Blütengrund.

Und sie empfingen ihn, den Makellosen,
in ihrem Leib, der ihre Seele war.
Und ihre Augen schlossen sich wie Rosen,
und voller Liebesnächte war ihr Haar.

Und ihn empfing das Große und Geringe.
Zu vielen Tieren kamen Cherubim
zu sagen, daß ihr Weibchen Früchte bringe,—
und waren wunderschöne Schmetterlinge:
denn ihn erkannten alle Dinge
und hatten Fruchtbarkeit aus ihm.

Und als er starb, so leicht wie ohne Namen,
da war er ausgeteilt: sein Samen rann
in Bächen, in den Bäumen sang sein Samen
und sah ihn ruhig aus den Blumen an.
Er lag und sang. Und als die Schwestern kamen,
da weinten sie um ihren lieben Mann.

29. Die Engel

Sie haben alle müde Münde
und helle Seelen ohne Saum.
Und eine Sehnsucht (wie nach Sünde)
geht ihnen manchmal durch den Traum.

Fast gleichen sie einander alle;
in Gottes Gärten schweigen sie,
wie viele, viele Intervalle
in seiner Macht und Melodie.

Nur wenn sie ihre Flügel breiten,
sind sie die Wecker eines Winds:

and silence fell over the nests,
and in the sisters, whom he touched
like a bridegroom, only their hearts cried out.

But then the pollen of his song
detached itself quietly from his red lips
and drifted dreamily to those loving ones
and fell into their open corollas
and slowly sank onto their pistils.

And they received him, the spotless one,
in their body, which was their soul.
And their eyes closed like roses,
and their hair was full of nights of love.

And great and small received him.
Cherubim came to many animals
to tell them that their mates were carrying young—
and they were wondrously beautiful butterflies:
for all things recognized him
and had fertility from him.

And when he died, as easily as if he were nameless,
he was distributed:[2] his seed flowed
in brooks, in the trees his seed sang,
beholding him calmly from the blossoms.
He lay there and sang. And when the sisters came
they wept over their beloved husband.

29. The Angels

They all have weary mouths
and bright, seamless souls.
And a longing (as if for sin)
sometimes passes through their dreams.

They all nearly look alike;
in God's garden they are silent,
like many, many intervals
in his might and melody.

Only when they spread their wings
are they the awakeners of a wind:

---

[2]No doubt an allusion to the distribution, or dispensation, of the Eucharist at Communion.

als ginge Gott mit seinen weiten
Bildhauerhänden durch die Seiten
im dunklen Buch des Anbeginns.

30. Der Schutzengel

Du bist der Vogel, dessen Flügel kamen,
wenn ich erwachte in der Nacht und rief.
Nur mit den Armen rief ich, denn dein Namen
ist wie ein Abgrund, tausend Nächte tief.
Du bist der Schatten, drin ich still entschlief,
und jeden Traum ersinnt in mir dein Samen,—
du bist das Bild, ich aber bin der Rahmen,
der dich ergänzt in glänzendem Relief.

Wie nenn ich dich? Sieh, meine Lippen lahmen.
Du bist der Anfang, der sich groß ergießt,
ich bin das langsame und bange Amen,
das deine Schönheit scheu beschließt.

Du hast mich oft aus dunklem Ruhn gerissen,
wenn mir das Schlafen wie ein Grab erschien
und wie Verlorengehen und Entfliehn,—
da hobst du mich aus Herzensfinsternissen
und wolltest mich auf allen Türmen hissen
wie Scharlachfahnen und wie Draperien.

Du: der von Wundern redet wie vom Wissen
und von den Menschen wie von Melodien
und von den Rosen: von Ereignissen,
die flammend sich in deinem Blick vollziehn,—
du Seliger, wann nennst du einmal Ihn,
aus dessen siebentem und letztem Tage
noch immer Glanz auf deinem Flügelschlage
verloren liegt . . .
Befiehlst du, daß ich frage?

31. Martyrinnen

Martyrin ist sie. Und als harten Falls
mit einem Ruck

as if God with his broad sculptor's hands
were leafing through the pages
of the obscure book of beginnings.

30. The Guardian Angel

You are the bird whose wings came
whenever I awoke at night and called.
I called with my arms only, because your name
is like an abyss a thousand nights deep.
Your are the shade in which I calmly fell asleep,
and your seed contrives every dream in me—
you are the picture, but I am the frame
that complements you in shining relievo.

What name shall I give you? See, my lips are numb.
You are the beginning that pours itself out voluminously,
I am the slow, frightened amen
that timidly concludes your beauty.

Often you have torn me out of obscure repose,
when sleep seemed like a grave to me
and like going astray and escaping—
then you raised me out of eclipses of the heart
and deigned to hoist me atop every tower
like scarlet banners and like festive hangings.

You who speak of miracles as if of ordinary knowledge
and of people as if of melodies
and of roses: of events
that blazingly take place in your eyes—
you blessed one, when will you finally name *him*
from whose seventh and final day
a glow even now lies lost
on your beating wings?. . .
Do you order me to ask?

31. Female Martyrs

She is a martyr. And when, falling heavily
with one jerk,

das Beil durch ihre kurze Jugend ging,
da legte sich der feine rote Ring
um ihren Hals, und war der erste Schmuck,
den sie mit einem fremden Lächeln nahm;
aber auch den erträgt sie nur mit Scham.
Und wenn sie schläft, muß ihre junge Schwester
(die, kindisch noch, sich mit der Wunde schmückt
von jenem Stein, der ihr die Stirn erdrückt)
die harten Arme um den Hals ihr halten,
und oft im Traume fleht die andre: Fester, fester.
Und da fällt es dem Kinde manchmal ein,
die Stirne mit dem Bild von jenem Stein
zu bergen in des sanften Nachtgewandes Falten,
das von der Schwester Atmen hell sich hebt,
voll wie ein Segel, das vom Winde lebt.

Das ist die Stunde, da sie heilig sind,
die stille Jungfrau und das blasse Kind.

Da sind sie wieder wie vor allem Leide
und schlafen arm und haben keinen Ruhm,
und ihre Seelen sind wie weiße Seide,
und von derselben Sehnsucht beben beide
und fürchten sich vor ihrem Heldentum.

Und du kannst meinen: wenn sie aus den Betten
aufstünden bei dem nächsten Morgenlichte
und, mit demselben träumenden Gesichte,
die Gassen kämen in den kleinen Städten,—
es bliebe keiner hinter ihnen staunen,
kein Fenster klirrte an den Häuserreihn,
und nirgends bei den Frauen ging ein Raunen,
und keines von den Kindern würde schrein.
Sie schritten durch die Stille in den Hemden
(die flachen Falten geben keinen Glanz)
so fremd, und dennoch keinem zum Befremden,
so wie zu Festen, aber ohne Kranz.

32. Kindheit

Da rinnt der Schule lange Angst und Zeit
mit Warten hin, mit lauter dumpfen Dingen.

the axe traversed her brief youth,
that delicate red circle placed itself
around her neck and was the first adornment
she ever accepted, with a strange smile,
but even it she endures only shamefacedly.
And when she sleeps, her young sister
(who, still childishly, adorns herself with the wound
made by that stone which crushed her forehead)
must keep her hard arms around her neck,
and often the other girl begs her while dreaming: "Tighter, tighter!"
And then it sometimes occurs to the child
to conceal her brow, with the imprint of that stone,
in the folds of the soft nightgown
that is lifted brightly by her sister's breathing,
filled like a sail that lives off the wind.

This is the hour when they are holy,
the calm virgin and the pale child.

Then they are once more as they were before any sorrow,
they sleep in poverty and enjoy no fame,
and their souls are like white silk,
and both tremble with the same longing
and are afraid of their own heroism.

And you might imagine: if they arose
from their beds in the next morning light
and, with the same dreaming faces,
walked down the streets of the small towns—
no one would be amazed at their passing,
no window in the rows of houses would rattle,
and nowhere would there be whispering among the women,
nor would any of the children cry out.
They would walk through the silence in their shifts
(the flat folds emit no shine)
so strangely, and yet astonishing no one,
as if for a feast day, but without a wreath.

32. Childhood

The lengthy anguish and time of school lessons
trickles by expectantly, filled merely with dull things.

O Einsamkeit, o schweres Zeitverbringen . . .
Und dann hinaus: die Straßen sprühn und klingen
und auf den Plätzen die Fontänen springen
und in den Gärten wird die Welt so weit—.
Und durch das alles gehn im kleinen Kleid,
ganz anders als die andern gehn und gingen—:
O wunderliche Zeit, o Zeitverbringen,
o Einsamkeit.

Und in das alles fern hinauszuschauen:
Männer und Frauen; Männer, Männer, Frauen
und Kinder, welche anders sind und bunt;
und da ein Haus und dann und wann ein Hund
und Schrecken lautlos wechselnd mit Vertrauen—:
O Trauer ohne Sinn, o Traum, o Grauen,
o Tiefe ohne Grund.

Und so zu spielen: Ball und Ring und Reifen
in einem Garten, welcher sanft verblaßt,
und manchmal die Erwachsenen zu streifen,
blind und verwildert in des Haschens Hast,
aber am Abend still, mit kleinen steifen
Schritten nachhaus zu gehn, fest angefaßt—:
O immer mehr entweichendes Begreifen,
o Angst, o Last.

Und stundenlang am großen grauen Teiche
mit einem kleinen Segelschiff zu knien;
es zu vergessen, weil noch andre, gleiche
und schönere Segel durch die Ringe ziehn,
und denken müssen an das kleine bleiche
Gesicht, das sinkend aus dem Teiche schien—:
O Kindheit, o entgleitende Vergleiche.
Wohin? Wohin?

33. Aus einer Kindheit

Das Dunkeln war wie Reichtum in dem Raume,
darin der Knabe, sehr verheimlicht, saß.
Und als die Mutter eintrat wie im Traume,
erzitterte im stillen Schrank ein Glas.

Oh solitude, oh, that hard way to spend time!. . .
And then outside: the streets sparkle and resound
and in the squares fountains play
and in the gardens the world becomes so wide. —
And to pass through all of that in a little dress,
very differently from the way others go about and went about:
Oh, peculiar time, oh, the time spent,
oh, solitude!

And to gaze out distantly at all that:
men and women; men, men, women,
and children who are different and variegated;
and here a house and now and then a dog
and terror noiselessly alternating with confidence:
Oh, senseless grief, oh, dream, oh horror,
oh, bottomless depths!

And to play that way: ball and quoits and hoop
in a garden that is gently growing pallid,
and sometimes to brush against adults
while blindly running wild in the haste of a game of tag,
but in the evening to go home with small,
stiff paces, holding hands tightly:
Oh, ever more elusive comprehension,
oh, anguish, oh, burden!

And to kneel for hours by the big gray pond
with a little sailboat;
to forget it because yet other sails, the same
or more beautiful, are floating through the round ripples,
and to have to think about the small pale
face that appeared out of the pond as if sinking:
Oh, childhood, oh, comparisons that slip away!
Where to? Where to?

33. From a Childhood

Dusk was like riches in the room
in which the boy sat, quite concealed.
And when his mother entered as if in a dream,
a glass trembled in the quiet cabinet.

Sie fühlte, wie das Zimmer sie verriet,
und küßte ihren Knaben: Bist du hier? . . .
Dann schauten beide bang nach dem Klavier,
denn manchen Abend hatte sie ein Lied,
darin das Kind sich seltsam tief verfing.

Es saß sehr still. Sein großes Schauen hing
an ihrer Hand, die ganz gebeugt vom Ringe,
als ob sie schwer in Schneewehn ginge,
über die weißen Tasten ging.

34. Der Knabe

Ich möchte einer werden so wie die,
die durch die Nacht mit wilden Pferden fahren,
mit Fackeln, die gleich aufgegangnen Haaren
in ihres Jagens großem Winde wehn.
Vorn möcht ich stehen wie in einem Kahne,
groß und wie eine Fahne aufgerollt.
Dunkel, aber mit einem Helm von Gold,
der unruhig glänzt. Und hinter mir gereiht
zehn Männer aus derselben Dunkelheit
mit Helmen, die, wie meiner, unstät sind,
bald klar wie Glas, bald dunkel, alt und blind.
Und einer steht bei mir und bläst uns Raum
mit der Trompete, welche blitzt und schreit,
und bläst uns eine schwarze Einsamkeit,
durch die wir rasen wie ein rascher Traum:
Die Häuser fallen hinter uns ins Knie,
die Gassen biegen sich uns schief entgegen,
die Plätze weichen aus: wir fassen sie,
und unsre Rosse rauschen wie ein Regen.

35. Die Konfirmanden
(Paris, im Mai 1903)

In weißen Schleiern gehn die Konfirmanden
tief in das neue Grün der Gärten ein.
Sie haben ihre Kindheit überstanden,
und was jetzt kommt, wird anders sein.

She sensed how the room betrayed her presence,
and kissed her boy: "Are you in here?". . .
Then both looked timorously at the piano,
for on many evenings she had a song
in which the child got caught up unusually deeply.

He sat very quietly. His great gaze hung
on her hand, which, quite weighted down with her ring,
as if plodding heavily through snowdrifts,
moved over the white keys.

34. The Boy

I'd like to become like one of those
who travel through the night with wild horses,
with torches that like undone hair
blow in the strong wind of their speed.
I'd like to be out in front, as if on a boat,
big and unfurled like a banner.
Dark but with a helmet of gold
shining nervously. And in a row behind me
ten men formed of the same darkness
with helmets that are inconstant like mine,
now clear as glass, now dark, old, and blind.
And one man is beside me, blowing room for us
with his trumpet, which flashes and screams,
blowing a black solitude for us,
through which we dash like a rapid dream:
behind us the houses sink to their knees,
the streets bend themselves crooked to meet us,
the squares make way: we seize them
and our steeds clatter like a rainstorm.

35. The Confirmands
(Paris, May 1903)

In white veils the confirmands enter
deeply into the fresh green of the gardens.
They have survived their childhood,
and what now comes will be different.

O kommt es denn! Beginnt jetzt nicht die Pause,
das Warten auf den nächsten Stundenschlag?
Das Fest ist aus, und es wird laut im Hause,
und trauriger vergeht der Nachmittag . . .

Das war ein Aufstehn zu dem weißen Kleide
und dann durch Gassen ein geschmücktes Gehn
und eine Kirche, innen kühl wie Seide,
und lange Kerzen waren wie Alleen,
und alle Lichter schienen wie Geschmeide,
von feierlichen Augen angesehn.

Und es war still, als der Gesang begann:
Wie Wolken stieg er in der Wölbung an
und wurde hell im Niederfall; und linder
denn Regen fiel er in die weißen Kinder.
Und wie im Wind bewegte sich ihr Weiß,
und wurde leise bunt in seinen Falten
und schien verborgne Blumen zu enthalten—:
Blumen und Vögel, Sterne und Gestalten
aus einem alten fernen Sagenkreis.

Und draußen war ein Tag aus Blau und Grün
mit einem Ruf von Rot an hellen Stellen.
Der Teich entfernte sich in kleinen Wellen,
und mit dem Winde kam ein fernes Blühn
und sang von Gärten draußen vor der Stadt.

Es war, als ob die Dinge sich bekränzten,
sie standen licht, unendlich leicht besonnt;
ein Fühlen war in jeder Häuserfront,
und viele Fenster gingen auf und glänzten.

36. Der Nachbar

Fremde Geige, gehst du mir nach?
In wieviel fernen Städten schon sprach
deine einsame Nacht zu meiner?
Spielen dich hunderte? Spielt dich einer?

Giebt es in allen großen Städten
solche, die sich ohne dich

Oh, isn't it coming! Doesn't the pause begin now,
the waiting for the next striking of the hour?
The holiday is over, and the house becomes noisy,
and the afternoon passes by more sadly. . . .

There was an awakening to the white dress
and then an adorned procession through the streets
and a church, cool as silk inside,
and there were long tapers like avenues of trees,
and all the lights shone like jewels,
beheld by solemn eyes.

And it was quiet when the chant began:
Like clouds it rose in the vaulted ceiling
and became bright as it sank down; and more gently
than rain it fell upon the white-clad children.
And their whiteness stirred as if in a breeze,
and became softly colorful in its folds
and seemed to contain hidden flowers:
flowers and birds, stars and figures
from an old, faraway cycle of legends.

And, outside, it was a day of blue and green
with a shout of red in bright places.
The pond moved away in small waves,
and with the wind came a distant blossoming,
singing of gardens out there in the suburbs.

It was as if every object put on a garland;
they all stood brightly, in infinitely soft sunshine;
there was feeling in every house facade,
and many a window opened up and shone.

36. The Neighbor

Strange violin, are you pursuing me?
In how many distant cities has your
lonesome night already spoken to mine?
Are you played by hundreds? Are you played by one man?

Are there people in every big city
who, were it not for you,

schon in den Flüssen verloren hätten?
Und warum trifft es immer mich?

Warum bin ich immer der Nachbar derer,
die dich bange zwingen zu singen
und zu sagen: Das Leben ist schwerer
als die Schwere von allen Dingen.

37. Pont du Carrousel

Der blinde Mann, der auf der Brücke steht,
grau wie ein Markstein namenloser Reiche,
er ist vielleicht das Ding, das immer gleiche,
um das von fern die Sternenstunde geht,
und der Gestirne stiller Mittelpunkt.
Denn alles um ihn irrt und rinnt und prunkt.

Er ist der unbewegliche Gerechte,
in viele wirre Wege hingestellt;
der dunkle Eingang in die Unterwelt
bei einem oberflächlichen Geschlechte.

38. Herbsttag

Herr: es ist Zeit. Der Sommer war sehr groß.
Leg deinen Schatten auf die Sonnenuhren,
und auf den Fluren laß die Winde los.

Befiehl den letzten Früchten voll zu sein;
gieb ihnen noch zwei südlichere Tage,
dränge sie zur Vollendung hin und jage
die letzte Süße in den schweren Wein.

Wer jetzt kein Haus hat, baut sich keines mehr.
Wer jetzt allein ist, wird es lange bleiben,
wird wachen, lesen, lange Briefe schreiben
und wird in den Alleen hin und her
unruhig wandern, wenn die Blätter treiben.

would have already lost themselves in rivers?
And why does it always affect *me*?

Why am I always the neighbor of those
who timorously compel you to sing
and to say: "Life is heavier
than the heaviness of all things"?

37. Pont du Carrousel

The blind man standing on the bridge,
gray as a boundary stone of nameless realms,
is perhaps that ever unchanging thing
around which the sidereal hour revolves from afar,
and the still midpoint of the constellations.
Because everything wanders and flows and parades around him.

He is the immovably righteous man,
placed on many a confused path;
the dark entrance to the underworld
amid a superficial generation.

38. Autumn Day

Lord: it's time. The summer was very great.
Cast your shadow on the sundials,
and let the winds loose in the fields.

Command the last fruits to be full;
give them another two days that are more southerly,
urge them into fulfillment and drive
the final sweetness into the heavy wine.

Whoever has no house now will no longer build himself one.
Whoever is alone now will long remain so,
will stay awake, read, write long letters,
and will roam restlessly to and fro
in the avenues of trees when the leaves drift.

39. Abend in Skåne

Der Park ist hoch. Und wie aus einem Haus
tret ich aus seiner Dämmerung heraus
in Ebene und Abend. In den Wind,
denselben Wind, den auch die Wolken fühlen,
die hellen Flüsse und die Flügelmühlen,
die langsam mahlend stehn am Himmelsrand.
Jetzt bin auch ich ein Ding in seiner Hand,
das kleinste unter diesen Himmeln. — Schau:

Ist das Ein Himmel?:
       Selig lichtes Blau,
in das sich immer reinere Wolken drängen,
und drunter alle Weiß in Übergängen,
und drüber jenes dünne, große Grau,
warmwallend wie auf roter Untermalung,
und über allem diese stille Strahlung
sinkender Sonne.

       Wunderlicher Bau,
in sich bewegt und von sich selbst gehalten,
Gestalten bildend, Riesenflügel, Falten
und Hochgebirge vor den ersten Sternen
und plötzlich, da : ein Tor in solche Fernen,
wie sie vielleicht nur Vögel kennen . . .

40. Abend

Der Abend wechselt langsam die Gewänder,
die ihm ein Rand von alten Bäumen hält;
du schaust: und von dir scheiden sich die Länder,
ein himmelfahrendes und eins, das fällt;

und lassen dich, zu keinem ganz gehörend,
nicht ganz so dunkel wie das Haus, das schweigt,
nicht ganz so sicher Ewiges beschwörend
wie das, was Stern wird jede Nacht und steigt—

und lassen dir (unsäglich zu entwirrn)
dein Leben bang und riesenhaft und reifend,

39. Evening in Skåne

The park is tall. And as if from a house
I step out of its twilight
into plain and evening. Into the wind,
the same wind that the clouds, too, feel,
the bright rivers, and the windmills
that stand on the sky's edge, slowly grinding.
Now I, too, am a thing in its hand,
the smallest beneath these skies.—Look:

Is that *one* sky?
                    A blissfully bright blue,
into which purer and purer clouds push,
and, below, all whites in transitional tones,
and, above, that big, thin grayness,
warmly surging as if over a red priming,
and, above it all, this calm radiance
of the sinking sun.

                    A peculiar construction,
moving within itself and contained by itself,
forming figures, gigantic wings, folds,
and high mountains before the first stars,
and suddenly, there: a gateway at a distance so great
that perhaps only birds know of things so far away . . . .

40. Evening

The evening is slowly changing its clothes,
which are held for it by a rim of old trees;
you look, and before you the countrysides separate,
one soaring skyward and one falling;

and they leave you belonging wholly to neither one,
not quite as dark as the taciturn house,
not quite so surely swearing to eternity
as does that which nightly becomes a star and rises—

and they leave you (impossible to untangle)
with a life that is timorous, gigantic, and ripening,

so daß es, bald begrenzt und bald begreifend,
abwechselnd Stein in dir wird und Gestirn.

41. Ernste Stunde

Wer jetzt weint irgendwo in der Welt,
     ohne Grund weint in der Welt,
     weint über mich.

Wer jetzt lacht irgendwo in der Nacht,
     ohne Grund lacht in der Nacht,
     lacht mich aus.

Wer jetzt geht irgendwo in der Welt,
     ohne Grund geht in der Welt,
     geht zu mir.

Wer jetzt stirbt irgendwo in der Welt,
     ohne Grund stirbt in der Welt:
     sieht mich an.

42. In der Certosa

Ein jeder aus der weißen Bruderschaft
vertraut sich pflanzend seinem kleinen Garten.
Auf jedem Beete steht, wer jeder sei.
Und Einer harrt in heimlichen Hoffahrten,
daß ihm im Mai
die ungestümen Blüten offenbarten
ein Bild von seiner unterdrückten Kraft.

Und seine Hände halten, wie erschlafft,
sein braunes Haupt, das schwer ist von den Säften,
die ungeduldig durch das Dunkel rollen,
und sein Gewand, das faltig, voll und wollen,
zu seinen Füßen fließt, ist stramm gestrafft
um seinen Armen, die, gleich starken Schäften,
die Hände tragen, welche träumen sollen.

Kein Miserere und kein Kyrie
will seine junge, runde Stimme ziehn,

so that, now circumscribed and now comprehending, it
becomes alternately stone and star within you.

41. Serious Hour

Whoever now weeps anywhere in the world,
      weeps groundlessly in the world,
      weeps over me.

Whoever now laughs anywhere in the night,
      laughs groundlessly in the night,
      mocks at me.

Whoever now journeys anywhere in the world,
      journeys groundlessly in the world,
      journeys to me.

Whoever now dies anywhere in the world,
      dies groundlessly in the world,
      looks at me.

42. In the Italian Carthusian Monestery

Each one of the white-habited brotherhood
entrusts himself as a planter to his little garden.
On every bed is written who each one is.
And one man persists in the secret vainglory
that in the spring
the tempestuous flowers will vouchsafe to him
an image of his repressed strength.

And his hands, as if grown limp, hold
his brown-haired head, which is heavy with the plant juices
that impatiently roll through the darkness,
and his robe, which, creased, full, and woolen,
flows to his feet, is tightly gathered
around his arms, which, like strong tree trunks,
carry his hands, which shall dream.

No Miserere and no Kyrie
is his full young voice willing to recite;

vor keinem Fluche will sie fliehn:
sie ist kein Reh.
Sie ist ein Roß und bäumt sich im Gebiß,
und über Hürde, Hang und Hindernis
will sie ihn tragen, weit und weggewiß,
ganz ohne Sattel will sie tragen ihn.

Er aber sitzt, und unter den Gedanken
zerbrechen fast die breiten Handgelenke,
so schwer wird ihm der Sinn und immer schwerer.

Der Abend kommt, der sanfte Wiederkehrer,
ein Wind beginnt, die Wege werden leerer,
und Schatten sammeln sich im Talgesenke.

Und wie ein Kahn, der an der Kette schwankt,
so wird der Garten ungewiß und hangt
wie windgewiegt auf lauter Dämmerung.
Wer löst ihn los ? . . .

Der Frate ist so jung,
und langelang ist seine Mutter tot.
Er weiß von ihr: sie nannten sie *La Stanca;*
sie war ein Glas, ganz zart und klar. Man bot
es einem, der es nach dem Trunk zerschlug
wie einen Krug.

So ist der Vater.
Und er hat sein Brot
als Meister in den roten Marmorbrüchen.
Und jede Wöchnerin in Pietrabianca
hat Furcht, daß er des Nachts mit seinen Flüchen
vorbei an ihrem Fenster kommt und droht.

Sein Sohn, den er der Donna Dolorosa
geweiht in einer Stunde wilder Not,
sinnt im Arkadenhofe der Certosa,
sinnt, wie umrauscht von rötlichen Gerüchen:
denn seine Blumen blühen alle rot.

43. Der Sohn

Mein Vater war ein verbannter
König von überm Meer.

it refuses to flee from any curse:
it's no roe deer.
It's a charger, rearing up and champing at the bit,
and over hurdles, slopes, and obstacles
it wants to carry him, far and certain of the way;
it wants to carry him without any saddle at all.

But he sits, and beneath the weight of his thoughts
his broad wrists nearly break,
so heavy and increasingly heavy does his mind become.

Evening arrives, that gentle returner,
a wind springs up, the roads become emptier,
and shadows gather in the hollow of the valley.

And like a boat rocking on its chain
the garden becomes indistinct and hangs,
as if wind-cradled, on sheer twilight.
Who will untie it? . . .

The friar is so young,
and his mother died ever so long ago.
All he knows about her is: she was called "the weary one";
she was a glass, very fragile and clear. It was offered
to a man who, after drinking from it, shattered it
like a pitcher.

That's what his father's like.
And he earns his bread
as a master workman in the red marble quarries.
And every woman in childbed in Pietrablanca
is afraid that he might pass by her window at night
with his curses and threats.

His son, whom he dedicated to the Lady of Sorrows
in an hour of wild distress,
broods in the arcaded yard of the monastery,
broods as if reddish fragrances were roaring around him:
for all his flowers turn out red.

43. The Son

My father was an exiled
king from over the sea.

Ihm kam einmal ein Gesandter:
sein Mantel war ein Panther,
und sein Schwert war schwer.

Mein Vater war wie immer
ohne Helm und Hermelin;
es dunkelte das Zimmer
wie immer arm um ihn.
Es zitterten seine Hände
und waren blaß und leer,—
in bilderlose Wände
blicklos schaute er.

Die Mutter ging im Garten
und wandelte weiß im Grün,
und wollte den Wind erwarten
vor dem Abendglühn.
Ich träumte, sie würde mich rufen,
aber sie ging allein,—
ließ mich vom Rande der Stufen
horchen verhallenden Hufen
und ins Haus hinein:

Vater! Der fremde Gesandte . . . ?
Der reitet wieder im Wind . . .
Was wollte der? Er erkannte
dein blondes Haar, mein Kind.
Vater! Wie war er gekleidet!
Wie der Mantel von ihm floß!
Geschmiedet und geschmeidet
war Schulter, Brust und Roß.
Er war eine Stimme im Stahle,
er war ein Mann aus Nacht,—
aber er hat eine schmale
Krone mitgebracht.
Sie klang bei jedem Schritte
an sein sehr schweres Schwert,
die Perle in ihrer Mitte
ist viele Leben wert.
Vom zornigen Ergreifen
verbogen ist der Reifen,
der oft gefallen war:

Once an envoy came to him:
his mantle was a panther
and his sword was heavy.

As always, my father was
without helmet or ermine;
as always, the room
was indigently dark around him.
His hands were trembling
and were pale and empty—
unseeing, he looked at
the pictureless walls.

My mother was walking in the garden,
a white figure roaming in the green,
and wanted to await the wind
before the glow of sunset.
I dreamed that she'd call to me,
but she walked by herself—
leaving me to listen, from the edge of the stairs,
to dying hoofbeats
and the events inside the house:

"Father! The foreign envoy. . . ?
He's riding again in the wind. . . .
What did he want?" "He recognized
your blond hair, my child."
"Father! The way he was dressed!
How his mantle flowed from him!
There was armor and jewelry
on his shoulders, breast, and steed.
He was a voice in the steel,
he was a man formed of night—
but he brought along
a narrow crown.
At every step it rang out
against his very heavy sword;
the pearl in its center
is worth many lives.
Its hoop is bent
from being gripped angrily,
and it had often fallen:

es ist eine Kinderkrone,—
denn Könige sind ohne;
—gieb sie meinem Haar!
Ich will sie manchmal tragen
in Nächten, blaß vor Scham.
Und will dir, Vater, sagen,
woher der Gesandte kam.
Was dort die Dinge gelten,
ob steinern steht die Stadt,
oder ob man in Zelten
mich erwartet hat.

Mein Vater war ein Gekränkter
und kannte nur wenig Ruh.
Er hörte mir mit verhängter
Stirne nächtelang zu.
Mir lag im Haar der Ring.
Und ich sprach ganz nahe und sachte,
daß die Mutter nicht erwachte,—
die an dasselbe dachte,
wenn sie, ganz weiß gelassen,
vor abendlichen Massen
durch dunkle Gärten ging.

                    *

. . . So wurden wir verträumte Geiger,
die leise aus den Türen treten,
um auszuschauen, eh sie beten,
ob nicht ein Nachbar sie belauscht.
Die erst, wenn alle sich zerstreuten,
hinter dem letzten Abendläuten,
die Lieder spielen, hinter denen
(wie Wald im Wind hinter Fontänen)
der dunkle Geigenkasten rauscht.
Denn dann nur sind die Stimmen gut,
wenn Schweigsamkeiten sie begleiten,
wenn hinter dem Gespräch der Saiten
Geräusche bleiben wie von Blut;
und bang und sinnlos sind die Zeiten,
wenn hinter ihren Eitelkeiten
nicht etwas waltet, welches ruht.

Geduld: es kreist der leise Zeiger,
und was verheißen ward, wird sein:

it's a child's crown—
for kings are without one—
bestow it on my hair!
I shall sometimes wear it
at night, pale with shame.
And, father, I shall tell you
where the envoy came from.
What the value of things is there,
whether the city's built of stone,
or whether I was awaited
in tents."

My father was an offended man
and knew very little rest.
He listened to me for entire nights
with a clouded brow.
The circlet lay on my hair.
And I spoke very close and softly,
so as not to awaken my mother—
who was thinking of the same thing
whenever, dressed all in white,
she'd walk through dark gardens
in front of masses of evening.

✲

. . . And so we became dreaming fiddlers
who softly step out of the doorways
to look and see, before they pray,
whether a neighbor isn't listening to them;
who only after all have dispersed,
after the last sounds of evening,
play the songs behind which
(like the forest in the wind behind fountains)
the dark body of the violin resounds:
For voices are only good
when accompanied by silences,
when beneath the conversation of the strings
there remain sounds like those of the blood;
and the times are frightened and meaningless
when beneath their vanities
there doesn't prevail something that is in repose.

Patience! The gentle minute-hand makes its rounds,
and that which was promised will occur:

Wir sind die Flüstrer vor dem Schweiger,
wir sind die Wiesen vor dem Hain;
in ihnen geht noch dunkles Summen—
(viel Stimmen sind und doch kein Chor)
und sie bereiten auf die stummen
tiefen heiligen Haine vor . . .

44. Die aus dem Hause Colonna

Ihr fremden Männer, die ihr jetzt so still
in Bildern steht, ihr saßet gut zu Pferde
und ungeduldig gingt ihr durch das Haus;
wie ein schöner Hund, mit derselben Gebärde
ruhn eure Hände jetzt bei euch aus.

Euer Gesicht ist so voll von Schauen,
denn die Welt war euch Bild und Bild;
aus Waffen, Fahnen, Früchten und Frauen
quillt euch dieses große Vertrauen,
daß alles *ist* und daß alles *gilt*.

Aber damals, als ihr noch zu jung
wart, die großen Schlachten zu schlagen,
zu jung, um den päpstlichen Purpur zu tragen,
nicht immer glücklich bei Reiten und Jagen,
Knaben noch, die sich den Frauen versagen,
habt ihr aus jenen Knabentagen
keine, nicht eine Erinnerung?

Wißt ihr nicht mehr, was damals war?

Damals war der Altar
mit dem Bilde, auf dem Maria gebar,
in dem einsamen Seitenschiff.
Euch ergriff
eine Blumenranke;
der Gedanke,
daß die Fontäne allein
draußen im Garten in Mondenschein
ihre Wasser warf,
war wie eine Welt.

We are the whisperers in the presence of the silent one,
we are the meadows in the presence of the grove;
in them obscure humming can still be heard
(there are many voices but they don't form a choir)
and they are a preparation for the mute,
deep, sacred groves. . . .

44. Those from the House of Colonna

You strange men, who now so calmly
stand in paintings, you sat your horse well
and paced through the house impatiently;
like a beautiful dog, with the same gesture
your hands are now at rest with you.

Your faces are so full of gazing,
for to you the world was picture after picture;
from weapons, banners, fruits, and women
stemmed that great conviction of yours
that everything *exists* and has *validity*.

But back then, when you were still
too young to fight the great battles,
too young to wear the papal purple,
not always fortunate in riding and hunting,
still boys who deny themselves to women,
have you no recollection from those
boyhood days, not one?

Do you no longer know what those days were like?

Back then the altar
with the picture showing Mary in childbed
stood in the lonely side aisle of the church.
Your emotions were stirred
by a blossoming tendril;
the thought
that the fountain alone
out in the garden in the moonlight
spurted its water
was like a world.

Das Fenster ging bis zu den Füßen auf wie eine Tür;
und es war Park mit Wiesen und Wegen:
seltsam nah und doch so entlegen,
seltsam hell und doch wie verborgen,
und die Brunnen rauschten wie Regen,
und es war, als käme kein Morgen
dieser langen Nacht entgegen,
die mit allen Sternen stand.

Damals wuchs euch, Knaben, die Hand,
die warm war. (Ihr aber wußtet es nicht.)
Damals breitete euer Gesicht sich aus.

45. Von den Fontänen

Auf einmal weiß ich viel von den Fontänen,
den unbegreiflichen Bäumen aus Glas.
Ich könnte reden wie von eignen Tränen,
die ich, ergriffen von sehr großen Träumen,
einmal vergeudete und dann vergaß.

Vergaß ich denn, daß Himmel Hände reichen
zu vielen Dingen und in das Gedränge?
Sah ich nicht immer Großheit ohnegleichen
im Aufstieg alter Parke, vor den weichen
erwartungsvollen Abenden, — in bleichen
aus fremden Mädchen steigenden Gesängen,
die überfließen aus der Melodie
und wirklich werden und als müßten sie
sich spiegeln in den aufgetanen Teichen?

Ich muß mich nur erinnern an das Alles,
was an Fontänen und an mir geschah,—
dann fühl ich auch die Last des Niederfalles,
in welcher ich die Wasser wiedersah:
Und weiß von Zweigen, die sich abwärts wandten,
von Stimmen, die mit kleiner Flamme brannten,
von Teichen, welche nur die Uferkanten
schwachsinnig und verschoben wiederholten,
von Abendhimmeln, welche von verkohlten
westlichen Wäldern ganz entfremdet traten

The window opened down to your feet like a door;
and there was the park with meadows and paths:
strangely near and yet so remote,
strangely bright and yet as if concealed,
and the springs babbled like rain,
and it was as if no morning would ever
confront that long night,
which was decked with every star.

Back then, boys, your hands grew,
and they were warm. (But you didn't know that.)
Back then your faces became broad.

45. Of the Fountains

All at once I knew a lot about the fountains,
those incomprehensible trees made of glass.
I could speak as if about my own tears,
which, stirred by very great dreams, I
once squandered and then forgot.

Did I, then, forget that heavens hold out hands
to many things and into the bustling crowd?
Didn't I always see incomparable greatness
in the rising ground of old parks, before the soft,
expectant evenings—in pale
songs ascending from unknown girls,
songs flowing over out of their melody
and becoming actual, as if they had to
be reflected in the ponds that had opened themselves?

I need only remember all the things
that befell the fountains and me—
then I also feel that burden of downfall
in which I saw the waters again:
And I know of branches that twisted downward;
of voices that burned with a small flame;
of ponds that merely repeated
the edges of their backs idiotically, dislocated,
of evening skies that stepped forth, quite estranged
by charred westerly woods,

sich anders wölbten, dunkelten und taten
als wär das nicht die Welt, die sie gemeint . . .

Vergaß ich denn, daß Stern bei Stern versteint
und sich verschließt gegen die Nachbargloben?
Daß sich die Welten nur noch wie verweint
im Raum erkennen? — Vielleicht sind wir *oben*,
in Himmel andrer Wesen eingewoben,
die zu uns aufschaun abends. Vielleicht loben
uns ihre Dichter. Vielleicht beten viele
zu uns empor. Vielleicht sind wir die Ziele
von fremden Flüchen, die uns nie erreichen,
Nachbaren eines Gottes, den sie meinen
in unsrer Höhe, wenn sie einsam weinen,
an den sie glauben und den sie verlieren,
und dessen Bildnis, wie ein Schein aus ihren
suchenden Lampen, flüchtig und verweht,
über unsere zerstreuten Gesichter geht . . . .

46. Der Schauende

Ich sehe den Bäumen die Stürme an,
die aus laugewordenen Tagen
an meine ängstlichen Fenster schlagen,
und höre die Fernen Dinge sagen,
die ich nicht ohne Freund ertragen,
nicht ohne Schwester lieben kann.

Da geht der Sturm, ein Umgestalter,
geht durch den Wald und durch die Zeit,
und alles ist wie ohne Alter:
die Landschaft, wie ein Vers im Psalter,
ist Ernst und Wucht und Ewigkeit.

Wie ist das klein, womit wir ringen,
was mit uns ringt, wie ist das groß;
ließen wir, ähnlicher den Dingen,
uns *so* vom großen Sturm bezwingen,—
wir würden weit und namenlos.

Was wir besiegen, ist das Kleine,
und der Erfolg selbst macht uns klein.

changed their vaulting, grew dark, and acted
as if that weren't the world they had imagined. . . .

Did I, then, forget that star after star turns to stone
and shuts itself off from its neighboring globes?
That the worlds now recognize one another in space
only as if with tear-stained eyes? Perhaps we are up there,
interwoven into what are skies to different beings
who look up to us in the evening. Perhaps their poets
praise us. Perhaps many send their prayers
upward to us. Perhaps we are the goals
of strange curses that never reach us,
neighbors of a God whom they conceive
to exist at our level when they weep in solitude,
in whom they believe and whom they lose,
and whose portrait, like a shine from their
searching lamps, fleeting and extinguished,
wanders over our distracted faces. . . .

46. The Gazer

I see on the trees the traces of the storms
that from days that have grown warm
beat on my anguished windows,
and I hear the distances saying things
that I can't bear without a friend,
can't love without a sister.

There the storm moves on, a thing that transforms,
moves on through the woods and through time,
and everything is as if ageless:
the landscape, like a verse in the psalm book,
is earnestness and gravity and eternity.

How small is that with which we struggle!
That which struggles with us—how big it is!
If, more similar to the things, we allowed
ourselves to be overcome *that way* by the great storm—
we'd become extensive and inexpressible.

What we conquer is trivial,
and our very success diminishes us.

Das Ewige und Ungemeine
will nicht von uns gebogen sein.
Das ist der Engel, der den Ringern
des Alten Testaments erschien:
wenn seiner Widersacher Sehnen
im Kampfe sich metallen dehnen,
fühlt er sie unter seinen Fingern
wie Saiten tiefer Melodien.

Wen dieser Engel überwand,
welcher so oft auf Kampf verzichtet,
der geht gerecht und aufgerichtet
und groß aus jener harten Hand,
die sich, wie formend, an ihn schmiegte.
Die Siege laden ihn nicht ein.
Sein Wachstum ist: der Tiefbesiegte
von immer Größerem zu sein.

47. Schlußstück

Der Tod ist groß.
Wir sind die Seinen
lachenden Munds.
Wenn wir uns mitten im Leben meinen,
wagt er zu weinen
mitten in uns.

48. Früher Apollo

Wie manches Mal durch das noch unbelaubte
Gezweig ein Morgen durchsieht, der schon ganz
im Frühling ist: so ist in seinem Haupte
nichts was verhindern könnte, daß der Glanz

aller Gedichte uns fast tödlich träfe;
denn noch kein Schatten ist in seinem Schaun,
zu kühl für Lorbeer sind noch seine Schläfe
und später erst wird aus den Augenbraun

hochstämmig sich der Rosengarten heben,
aus welchem Blätter, einzeln, ausgelöst
hintreiben werden auf des Mundes Beben,

The eternal and unusual
refuses to be bent by us.
It's the angel who affeared
to the Old Testament wrestlers:
whenever his opponents' sinews
stretch like metal in battle,
he feels them under his fingers
like strings producing profound melodies.

The man bested by this angel,
who so frequently renounces combat,
emerges as a righteous, erect,
and great man from that hard grip
which, as it were, shaped him while clinging to him.
Victories aren't inviting to him.
His growth is to be the one profoundly conquered
by something greater and greater.

47. Endpiece [to the *Book of Images*]

Death is mighty.
We belong to him
with laughing lips.
Whenever we think we are in the midst of life,
he is bold enough to weep
in the midst of us.

48. An Apollo of an Early Period

Just as a morning sometimes peeps through the still
leafless branches, a morning already altogether
partaking of Spring, similarly, in his heat
there's nothing that could prevent the glow

of all poetry from wounding us almost mortally;
for there's no shadow yet in his gaze,
his temples are still too cool for laurel,
and only later, out of his eyebrows, will

the tall-stemmed rose garden arise
from which individual, detached petals
will drift on his trembling lips,

der jetzt noch still ist, niegebraucht und blinkend
und nur mit seinem Läeheln etwas trinkend
als würde ihm sein Singen eingeflößt.

49. Liebes-Lied

Wie soll ich meine Seele halten, daß
sie nicht an deine rührt? Wie soll ich sie
hinheben über dich zu andern Dingen?
Ach gerne möcht ich sie bei irgendwas
Verlorenem im Dunkel unterbringen
an einer fremden stillen Stelle, die
nicht weiterschwingt, wenn deine Tiefen schwingen.
Doch alles, was uns anrührt, dich und mich,
nimmt uns zusammen wie ein Bogenstrich,
der aus zwei Saiten *eine* Stimme zieht.
Auf welches Instrument sind wir gespannt?
Und welcher Geiger hat uns in der Hand?
O süßes Lied.

50. Opfer

O wie blüht mein Leib aus jeder Ader
duftender, seitdem ich dich erkenn;
sieh, ich gehe schlanker und gerader,
und du wartest nur —: wer bist du denn?

Sieh: ich fühle, wie ich mich entferne,
wie ich Altes, Blatt um Blatt, verlier.
Nur dein Lächeln steht wie lauter Sterne
über dir und bald auch über mir.

Alles was durch meine Kinderjahre
namenlos noch und wie Wasser glänzt,
will ich nach dir nennen am Altare,
der entzündet ist von deinem Haare
und mit deinen Brüsten leicht bekränzt.

which are now still quiet, unused, and gleaming,
and merely drinking something in through their smile,
as if their song were being infused into them.

49. Love Song

How am I to restrain my soul, to keep it
from touching yours? How am I to
raise it beyond you to other things?
Ah, I'd gladly lodge it with something
that's lost in the darkness
in a strange, quiet place which
didn't keep on vibrating when your depths vibrate.
But everything that touches us, you and me,
joins us together like the bowing of a violin
that elicits a single voice from two strings.
On what instrument are we strung?
And what violinist holds us in his hand?
Oh, sweet song!

50. Offering

Oh, how my body has blossomed more fragrantly
from each vein ever since I've recognized you!
See, I go about slimmer and straighter,
and you merely wait—who are you, then?

See: I feel myself moving into the distance,
losing old things, leaf after leaf.
Only your smile is there like sheer starlight
over you and soon over me, too.

Everything shining through my childhood years,
still unexpressed, and like water,
I want to name after you at the altar
that's ignited by your hair
and lightly garlanded with your breasts.

51. Östliches Taglied

Ist dieses Bette nicht wie eine Küste,
ein Küstenstreifen nur, darauf wir liegen?
Nichts ist gewiß als deine hohen Brüste,
die mein Gefühl in Schwindeln überstiegen.

Denn diese Nacht, in der so vieles schrie,
in der sich Tiere rufen und zerreißen,
ist sie uns nicht entsetzlich fremd? Und wie:
was draußen langsam anhebt, Tag geheißen,
ist das uns denn verständlicher als sie?

Man müßte so sich ineinanderlegen
wie Blütenblätter um die Staubgefäße:
so sehr ist überall das Ungemäße
und häuft sich an und stürzt sich uns entgegen.

Doch während wir uns aneinander drücken,
um nicht zu sehen, wie es ringsum naht,
kann es aus dir, kann es aus mir sich zücken:
denn unsre Seelen leben von Verrat.

52. Der Auszug des verlorenen Sohnes

Nun fortzugehn von alledem Verwornen,
das unser ist und uns doch nicht gehört,
das, wie das Wasser in den alten Bornen,
uns zitternd spiegelt und das Bild zerstört;
von allem diesen, das sich wie mit Dornen
noch einmal an uns anhängt—fortzugehn
und Das und Den,
die man schon nicht mehr sah
(so täglich waren sie und so gewöhnlich),
auf einmal anzuschauen: sanft, versöhnlich
und wie an einem Anfang und von nah;
und ahnend einzusehn, wie unpersönlich,
wie über alle hin das Leid geschah,
von dem die Kindheit voll war bis zum Rand—:
Und dann doch fortzugehen, Hand aus Hand,
als ob man ein Geheiltes neu zerrisse,

51. Eastern Aubade

Isn't this bed on which we lie
like a coast, merely a length of coastline?
Nothing is certain except your high breasts,
which my emotions have dizzily surmounted.

For this night, in which there were so many outcries,
in which animals call to, and rend, one another,
isn't it terribly strange to us? And also,
that which, named day, is slowly beginning outside,
is it really more comprehensible to us than the night?

We need to intertwine ourselves like this,
like flower petals around the stamens:
because disproportion is so ubiquitous,
and accumulating and plunging at us.

But while we press ourselves against each other
to avoid seeing how it approaches on all sides,
it may very well unsheathe itself from you, from me:
for our souls live on betrayal.

52. The Setting Out of the Prodigal Son

To depart now from all this confusion
which is ours and yet doesn't belong to us,
which, like the water in the old wells,
reflects us in a tremble, distorting our image;
from all this which, as if with brambles,
once again clings to us—to depart
and all at once to behold those things and persons
that we have already ceased to see
(they were so everyday and so ordinary):
to behold them in a gentle, conciliatory way
and as if at an outset and close up;
and to realize surmisingly how impersonal
the woe was that occurred, affecting everyone,
the woe that filled our childhood to the brim—
And then to depart all the same, hand loosed from hand,
as if tearing open a healed wound again,

und fortzugehn: wohin? Ins Ungewisse,
weit in ein unverwandtes warmes Land,
das hinter allem Handeln wie Kulisse
gleichgültig sein wird: Garten oder Wand;
und fortzugehn: warum? Aus Drang, aus Artung,
aus Ungeduld, aus dunkler Erwartung,
aus Unverständlichkeit und Unverstand:

Dies alles auf sich nehmen und vergebens
vielleicht Gehaltnes fallen lassen, um
allein zu sterben, wissend nicht warum—

Ist das der Eingang eines neuen Lebens?

53. Der Ölbaum-Garten

Er ging hinauf unter dem grauen Laub
ganz grau und aufgelöst im Ölgelände
und legte seine Stirne voller Staub
tief in das Staubigsein der heißen Hände.

Nach allem dies. Und dieses war der Schluß.
Jetzt soll ich gehen, während ich erblinde,
und warum willst Du, daß ich sagen muß
Du seist, wenn ich Dich selber nicht mehr finde.

Ich finde Dich nicht mehr. Nicht in mir, nein.
Nicht in den andern. Nicht in diesem Stein.
Ich finde Dich nicht mehr. Ich bin allein.

Ich bin allein mit aller Menschen Gram,
den ich durch Dich zu lindern unternahm,
der Du nicht bist. O namenlose Scham . . .

Später erzählte man: ein Engel kam—.

Warum ein Engel? Ach es kam die Nacht
und blätterte gleichgültig in den Bäumen.
Die Jünger rührten sich in ihren Träumen.
Warum ein Engel? Ach es kam die Nacht.

Die Nacht, die kam, war keine ungemeine;
so gehen hunderte vorbei.
Da schlafen Hunde und da liegen Steine.

and to depart: where? Into uncertainty,
far into an unrelated, hot country,
which, behind all our doings, will be indifferent
like a stage set: garden or wall.
And to depart: why? Out of an urge, a predisposition,
impatience, obscure expectations,
out of unintelligibility and thoughtlessness:

To take all this upon oneself and, in vain,
perhaps to let drop something one has held, in order
to die alone, not knowing why—

Is this the entry to a new life?

53. The Mount of Olives

He ascended beneath the gray foliage,
himself all gray and dissolved into the olive grove,
and placed his dust-covered forehead
deep in the dustiness of his hot hands.

After all that—this! And this was the end.
Now I am to go, while I grow blind,
and why do you want me to have to say
you exist when I no longer find you myself?

I no longer find you. Not in me, no.
Not in the others. Not in this stone.
I no longer find you. I am alone.

I am alone with the sorrow of all mankind,
which I undertook to solace through you,
you who don't exist. Oh, my unspeakable shame! . . .

Later, people told that an angel came. —

Why an angel? Ah, it was the night that came,
leafing indifferently through the trees.
The disciples stirred in their dreams.
Why an angel? Ah, it was the night that came.

The night that came was no unusual one;
hundreds of that sort go by.
During them, dogs sleep and stones lie there.

Ach eine traurige, ach irgendeine,
die wartet, bis es wieder Morgen sei.

Denn Engel kommen nicht zu solchen Betern,
und Nächte werden nicht um solche groß.
Die Sich-Verlierenden läßt alles los,
und sie sind preisgegeben von den Vätern
und ausgeschlossen aus der Mütter Schooß.

54. Gesang der Frauen an den Dichter

Sieh, wie sich alles auftut: so sind wir;
denn wir sind nichts als solche Seligkeit.
Was Blut und Dunkel war in einem Tier,
das wuchs in uns zur Seele an und schreit

als Seele weiter. Und es schreit nach dir.
Du freilich nimmst es nur in dein Gesicht
als sei es Landschaft: sanft und ohne Gier.
Und darum meinen wir, du bist es nicht,

nach dem es schreit. Und doch, bist du nicht der,
an den wir uns ganz ohne Rest verlören?
Und werden wir in irgend einem *mehr?*

Mit uns geht das Unendliche *vorbei.*
Du aber sei, du Mund, daß wir es hören,
du aber, du Uns-Sagender: du sei.

55. Gott im Mittelalter

Und sie hatten Ihn in sich erspart
und sie wollten, daß er sei und richte,
und sie hängten schließlich wie Gewichte
(zu verhindern seine Himmelfahrt)

an ihn ihrer großen Kathedralen
Last und Masse. Und er sollte nur
über seine grenzenlosen Zahlen
zeigend kreisen und wie eine Uhr

Zeichen geben ihrem Tun und Tagwerk.
Aber plötzlich kam er ganz in Gang,
und die Leute der entsetzten Stadt

Ah, a sad night, ah, an ordinary one,
one that waits till it's morning again.

For angels don't come to praying people of that sort,
nor do nights become great for the sake of such folk.
Everything abandons those who go astray,
and they are renounced by their fathers
and excluded from their mothers' bosom.

54. Song of the Women to the Poet

See how everything is opening up: we're like that;
for we are nothing but such bliss.
What was blood and darkness in an animal
developed in us into a soul and cries out

further as a soul. And it cries out for you.
You, of course, admit it to your sight merely
as if it were a landscape: gently, without craving.
And so we imagine that it isn't you

it's crying out for. And yet, aren't you the man
through whom we'd lose ourselves totally?
And do we become *more* in any other man?

With us infinity *passes by*.
But you, you lips: exist so we can hear it!
But you who tell of us: exist!

55. God in the Middle Ages

And they had stored him up in themselves
and they wanted him to exist and to judge,
and finally they hung up like weights
(to prevent his ascension to heaven)

upon him their great cathedrals'
burden and mass. And he was merely
to circle like a pointer over his limitless
numbers and, like a clock,

to give signals for their actions and daily work.
But suddenly he came into full motion,
and the people in the horrified city,

ließen ihn, vor seiner Stimme bang,
weitergehn mit ausgehängtem Schlagwerk
und entflohn vor seinem Zifferblatt.

56. Der Panther
Im Jardin des Plantes, Paris

Sein Blick ist vom Vorübergehn der Stäbe
so müd geworden, daß er nichts mehr hält.
Ihm ist, als ob es tausend Stäbe gäbe
und hinter tausend Stäben keine Welt.

Der weiche Gang geschmeidig starker Schritte,
der sich im allerkleinsten Kreise dreht,
ist wie ein Tanz von Kraft um eine Mitte,
in der betäubt ein großer Wille steht.

Nur manchmal schiebt der Vorhang der Pupille
sich lautlos auf —. Dann geht ein Bild hinein,
geht durch der Glieder angespannte Stille—
und hört im Herzen auf zu sein.

57. Das Einhorn

Der Heilige hob das Haupt, und das Gebet
fiel wie ein Helm zurück von seinem Haupte:
denn lautlos nahte sich das niegeglaubte,
das weiße Tier, das wie eine geraubte
hülflose Hindin mit den Augen fleht.

Der Beine elfenbeinernes Gestell
bewegte sich in leichten Gleichgewichten,
ein weißer Glanz glitt selig durch das Fell,
und auf der Tierstirn, auf der stillen, lichten,
stand, wie ein Turm im Mond, das Horn so hell,
und jeder Schritt geschah, es aufzurichten.

Das Maul mit seinem rosagrauen Flaum
war leicht gerafft, so daß ein wenig Weiß
(weißer als alles) von den Zähnen glänzte;
die Nüstern nahmen auf und lechzten leis.

fearing his voice, left him
go on with his mechanism exposed,
and they fled from his dial.

56. The Panther
In the Jardin des Plantes, Paris

From walking past the bars his eyes
have grown so tired, they retain nothing more.
It seems to him there are a thousand bars
and, behind those thousand bars, no world.

His soft walk, with lithe and strong steps,
turning in the smallest possible circle,
is like a dance of force around a midpoint
in which a mighty will stands benumbed.

Only at times is the curtain of his pupils
noiselessly raised. —Then an image enters,
passes through the tensed calm of his limbs—
and in his heart ceases to be.

57. The Unicorn

The saint lifted his head, and his prayer
fell back from his head like a helmet:
for noiselessly there approached the never-believed
white animal that beseeches with its eyes
like an abducted, helpless doe.

The ivory framework of its legs
moved in an easy equilibrium;
a white gleam ran blissfully over its hide,
and on the beast's brow, so quiet and bright,
stood, like a moonlit tower, the shining horn,
and every pace only made it more erect.

Its mouth, with its pinkish gray fluff,
was slightly curled, so that a little white
(whiter than anything) shone from its teeth;
its nostrils inhaled and panted gently.

Doch seine Blicke, die kein Ding begrenzte,
warfen sich Bilder in den Raum
und schlossen einen blauen Sagenkreis.

58. Der Schwan

Diese Mühsal, durch noch Ungetanes
schwer und wie gebunden hinzugehn,
gleicht dem ungeschaffnen Gang des Schwanes.

Und das Sterben, dieses Nichtmehrfassen
jenes Grunds, auf dem wir täglich stehn,
seinem ängstlichen Sich-Niederlassen—:

in die Wasser, die ihn sanft empfangen
und die sich, wie glücklich und vergangen,
unter ihm zurückziehn, Flut um Flut;
während er unendlich still und sicher
immer mündiger und königlicher
und gelassener zu ziehn geruht.

59. Tanagra

Ein wenig gebrannter Erde,
wie von großer Sonne gebrannt.
Als wäre die Gebärde
einer Mädchenhand
auf einmal nicht mehr vergangen;
ohne nach etwas zu langen,
zu keinem Dinge hin
aus ihrem Gefühle führend,
nur an sich selber rührend
wie eine Hand ans Kinn.

Wir heben und wir drehen
eine und eine Figur;
wir können fast verstehen
weshalb sie nicht vergehen,—

But its gazes, which nothing limited,
flung images through space to one another,
enclosing a blue legend-cycle.

58. The Swan

Our toilsome effort to traverse things yet undone
in heaviness, as if we were tied up,
is like the awkward[3] gait of the swan.

And our death, that inability to grasp any further
the ground on which we daily stand,
is like his anguished landing

on the water that receives him gently
and, as if happy and a thing of the past,
draws away beneath him wave after wave,
while, infinitely calm and sure,
he deigns to proceed more and more authoritatively,
royally, and sedately.

59. Tanagra

A little baked earth,
as if baked by strong sunlight.
As if the gesture
of a girl's hand
were all at once no more a thing of the past;
not reaching out for anything,
leading to no thing
out of her emotion,
merely touching herself
as one's hand touches one's chin.

We lift and turn
one figure after another;
we can almost understand
why they don't perish—

---

[3]Literally: "uncreated."

aber wir sollen nur
tiefer und wunderbarer
hängen an dem was war
und lächeln: ein wenig klarer
vielleicht als vor einem Jahr.

60. Die Erblindende

Sie saß so wie die anderen beim Tee.
Mir war zuerst, als ob sie ihre Tasse
ein wenig anders als die andern fasse.
Sie lächelte einmal. Es tat fast weh.

Und als man schließlich sich erhob und sprach
und langsam und wie es der Zufall brachte
durch viele Zimmer ging (man sprach und lachte),
da sah ich sie. Sie ging den andern nach,

verhalten, so wie eine, welche gleich
wird singen müssen und vor vielen Leuten;
auf ihren hellen Augen die sich freuten
war Licht von außen wie auf einem Teich.

Sie folgte langsam und sie brauchte lang
als wäre etwas noch nicht überstiegen;
und doch: als ob, nach einem Übergang,
sie nicht mehr gehen würde, sondern fliegen.

61. Jugend-Bildnis meines Vaters

Im Auge Traum. Die Stirn wie in Berührung
mit etwas Fernem. Um den Mund enorm
viel Jugend, ungelächelte Verführung,
und vor der vollen schmückenden Verschnürung
der schlanken adeligen Uniform
der Säbelkorb und beide Hände—, die
abwarten, ruhig, zu nichts hingedrängt.
Und nun fast nicht mehr sichtbar: als ob sie
zuerst, die Fernes greifenden, verschwänden.
Und alles andre mit sich selbst verhängt

but we should only
more deeply and wondrously
cling to that which has been,
and smile: a little more brightly,
perhaps, than a year ago.

60. The Woman Growing Blind

She sat at tea just like the others.
At first I thought she held her cup
a little differently from the others.
She smiled once. It was almost painful.

And when we finally arose and spoke
and slowly, and as chance brought it about,
roamed through many rooms (we spoke and laughed),
I saw her. She was following the others,

under a constraint, like a woman who will soon
have to sing, and in front of a big crowd;
on her bright eyes, which were joyful,
lay a light from without, as if on a pool.

She followed slowly and she needed a long time,
as if something were not yet surmounted;
and yet as if, after passing that obstacle,
she would no longer walk, but fly.

61. Portrait of My Father as a Young Man

In his eyes, dream. His forehead as if in contact
with something distant. Around his mouth an enormous
amount of youth, unobtrusive seductiveness,
and in front of the full, decorative frogging
of his slender, noble uniform
the saber shell and his two hands—in
calm expectancy, not thrust out at anything.
And now nearly no more visible: as if,
grasping remoteness, they were the first to disappear.
And all the rest concealed by itself

und ausgelöscht als ob wirs nicht verständen
und tief aus seiner eignen Tiefe trüb—.

Du schnell vergehendes Daguerreotyp
in meinen langsamer vergehenden Händen.

62. Selbstbildnis aus dem Jahre 1906

Des alten lange adligen Geschlechtes
Feststehendes im Augenbogenbau.
Im Blicke noch der Kindheit Angst und Blau
und Demut da und dort, nicht eines Knechtes
doch eines Dienenden und einer Frau.
Der Mund als Mund gemacht, groß und genau,
nicht überredend, aber ein Gerechtes
Aussagendes. Die Stirne ohne Schlechtes
und gern im Schatten stiller Niederschau.

Das, als Zusammenhang, erst nur geahnt;
noch nie im Leiden oder im Gelingen
zusammgefaßt zu dauerndem Durchdringen,
doch so, als wäre mit zerstreuten Dingen
von fern ein Ernstes, Wirkliches geplant.

63. Der letzte Graf von Brederode entzieht sich türkischer Gefangenschaft

Sie folgten furchtbar; ihren bunten Tod
von ferne nach ihm werfend, während er
verloren floh, nichts weiter als: bedroht.
Die Ferne seiner Väter schien nicht mehr

für ihn zu gelten; denn um so zu fliehn,
genügt ein Tier vor Jägern. Bis der Fluß
aufrauschte nah und blitzend. Ein Entschluß
hob ihn samt seiner Not und machte ihn

wieder zum Knaben fürstlichen Geblütes.
Ein Lächeln adeliger Frauen goß
noch einmal Süßigkeit in sein verfrühtes

and extinguished as if we didn't understand it
and deeply blurred out of its own profundity.

You rapidly decaying daguerreotype
in my more slowly decaying hands.

62. Self-Portrait from the Year 1906

The old long-noble lineage's
established firmness in the shape of my eyebrow ridge.
In my gaze the lingering anxiety and blueness of childhood,
and humility here and there, not that of a menial
and yet that of one who serves and of a woman.
The mouth shaped like a mouth, large and precise,
not persuasive but expressing
upright thoughts. The forehead with nothing bad in it
and gladly shaded by a calm glance downward.

All that, as an ensemble, merely surmised at first;
never yet in sorrow or in success
composed into a durable penetration,
but as if with scattered things
something earnest and real were being planned far off.

63. The Last Count of Brederode Escapes from Turkish Captivity

They pursued him frightfully; hurling their manifold death
at him from a distance, while he
fled forlorn, feeling no more than menaced.
His ancestors far away seemed no longer

to count for him; for to flee in that way,
to be a hunted animal suffices. Until the river
roared up, close by and flashing. A decision
uplifted him together with his distress and made him

once more a boy of princely blood.
A smile from ladies of nobility poured
sweetness again into his prematurely

vollendetes Gesicht. Er zwang sein Roß,
groß wie sein Herz zu gehn, sein blutdurchglühtes:
es trug ihn in den Strom wie in sein Schloß.

64. Römische Fontäne
Borghese

Zwei Becken, eins das andre übersteigend
aus einem alten runden Marmorrand,
und aus dem oberen Wasser leis sich neigend
zum Wasser, welches unten wartend stand,

dem leise redenden entgegenschweigend
und heimlich, gleichsam in der hohlen Hand,
ihm Himmel hinter Grün und Dunkel zeigend
wie einen unbekannten Gegenstand;

sich selber ruhig in der schönen Schale
verbreitend ohne Heimweh, Kreis aus Kreis,
nur manchmal träumerisch und tropfenweis

sich niederlasssend an den Moosbehängen
zum letzten Spiegel, der sein Becken leis
von unten lächeln macht mit Übergängen.

65. Das Karussell
Jardin du Luxembourg

Mit einem Dach und seinem Schatten dreht
sich eine kleine Weile der Bestand
von bunten Pferden, alle aus dem Land,
das lange zögert, eh es untergeht.
Zwar manche sind an Wagen angespannt,
doch alle haben Mut in ihren Mienen;
ein böser roter Löwe geht mit ihnen
und dann und wann ein weißer Elefant.

Sogar ein Hirsch ist da, ganz wie im Wald,
nur daß er einen Sattel trägt und drüber
ein kleines blaues Mädchen aufgeschnallt.

perfected face. He compelled his steed
to race as valiantly as his own red-glowing heart:
it bore him into the current as if into his castle.

64. Roman Fountain
Borghese

Two basins, one surmounting the other
as they emerge from an old circular marble rim,
and with a gentle incline from the upper water
to the water that stood waiting below,

meeting with silence the other's quiet speech
and secretly, as if in the hollow of one's hand,
showing it the sky, behind greenness and darkness,
like an unfamiliar object;

spreading itself calmly in its lovely bowl
without homesickness, circle issuing from circle,
only dreamy at times and drop by drop

settling past the tapestries of moss
onto the last reflecting surface, which softly makes its basin
smile from below with transitional images.

65. The Carousel
Jardin du Luxembourg

With a roof and its shadow
for a little while the stock
of colored horses turns, all from a land
that hesitates for a long time before it perishes.
To be sure, many are harnessed to carriages,
but they all have courage in their expressions;
a fierce red lion moves along with them
and now and then a white elephant.

There's even a stag there, just as in the woods,
except he wears a saddle and on top of it
a little blue-clad girl buckled on.

Und auf dem Löwen reitet weiß ein Junge
und hält sich mit der kleinen heißen Hand,
dieweil der Löwe Zähne zeigt und Zunge.

Und dann und wann ein weißer Elefant.

Und auf den Pferden kommen sie vorüber,
auch Mädchen, helle, diesem Pferdesprunge
fast schon entwachsen; mitten in dem Schwunge
schauen sie auf, irgendwohin, herüber—

Und dann und wann ein weißer Elefant.

Und das geht hin und eilt sich, daß es endet,
und kreist und dreht sich nur und hat kein Ziel.
Ein Rot, ein Grün, ein Grau vorbeigesendet,
ein kleines kaum begonnenes Profil—.
Und manchesmal ein Lächeln, hergewendet,
ein seliges, das blendet und verschwendet
an dieses atemlose blinde Spiel . . .

66. Spanische Tänzerin

Wie in der Hand ein Schwefelzündholz, weiß,
eh es zur Flamme kommt, nach allen Seiten
zuckende Zungen streckt—: beginnt im Kreis
naher Beschauer hastig, hell und heiß
ihr runder Tanz sich zuckend auszubreiten.

Und plötzlich ist er Flamme, ganz und gar.

Mit einem Blick entzündet sie ihr Haar
und dreht auf einmal mit gewagter Kunst
ihr ganzes Kleid in diese Feuersbrunst,
aus welcher sich, wie Schlangen die erschrecken,
die nackten Arme wach und klappernd strecken.

Und dann: als würde ihr das Feuer knapp,
nimmt sie es ganz zusamm und wirft es ab
sehr herrisch, mit hochmütiger Gebärde
und schaut: da liegt es rasend auf der Erde
und flammt noch immer und ergiebt sich nicht—.

And on the lion rides a boy dressed in white,
holding on with his little hot hand
while the lion shows its teeth and tongue.

And now and then a white elephant.

And on the horses they come by,
even gleaming girls who're almost too old
for this horse jumping; in mid-whirl
they look up, somewhere—in this direction—

And now and then a white elephant.

And all this passes and hastens to conclude,
and merely wheels and turns without a destination.
A red, a green, a gray flash by,
a little profile scarcely sketched. —
And at times a smile turned in this direction,
a blissful one that dazzles and spends itself
on this breathless, blind pastime. . . .

66. Flamenco Dancer

Just as a white sulfur match in one's hand,
before it bursts into flame, emits twitching tongues
in every direction: so, in the circle
of spectators close by, her circling dance
begins to spread itself out, bright, hot, twitching.

And suddenly it's entirely flame.

With a glance she ignites her hair
and all at once, with bold art, whirls
her whole dress into this conflagration,
from which, like frightened snakes,
her naked arms extend, alert and rattling.

And then: as if the fire were too snug for her,
she gathers it all up and casts it off
very imperiously, with a haughty gesture,
and gazes: there it lies raging on the floor,
still flaming, not surrendering. —

Doch sieghaft, sicher und mit einem süßen
grüßenden Lächeln hebt sie ihr Gesicht
und stampft es aus mit kleinen festen Füßen.

67. Orpheus. Eurydike. Hermes

Das war der Seelen wunderliches Bergwerk.
Wie stille Silbererze gingen sie
als Adern durch sein Dunkel. Zwischen Wurzeln
entsprang das Blut, das fortgeht zu den Menschen,
und schwer wie Porphyr sah es aus im Dunkel.
Sonst war nichts Rotes.

Felsen waren da
und wesenlose Wälder. Brücken über Leeres
und jener große graue blinde Teich,
der über seinem fernen Grunde hing
wie Regenhimmel über einer Landschaft.
Und zwischen Wiesen, sanft und voller Langmut,
erschien des einen Weges blasser Streifen,
wie eine lange Bleiche hingelegt.

Und dieses einen Weges kamen sie.

Voran der schlanke Mann im blauen Mantel,
der stumm und ungeduldig vor sich aussah.
Ohne zu kauen fraß sein Schritt den Weg
in großen Bissen; seine Hände hingen
schwer und verschlossen aus dem Fall der Falten
und wußten nicht mehr von der leichten Leier,
die in die Linke eingewachsen war
wie Rosenranken in den Ast des Ölbaums.
Und seine Sinne waren wie entzweit:
indes der Blick ihm wie ein Hund vorauslief,
umkehrte, kam und immer wieder weit
und wartend an der nächsten Wendung stand,—
blieb sein Gehör wie ein Geruch zurück.
Manchmal erschien es ihm als reichte es
bis an das Gehen jener beiden andern,
die folgen sollten diesen ganzen Aufstieg.
Dann wieder wars nur seines Steigens Nachklang

But victorious, confident, and with a sweet
smile of greeting, she raises her face
and stamps it out with small, firm feet.

67. Orpheus. Eurydice. Hermes

It was the strange mine of souls.
Like silent silver ore they extended
as veins through its darkness. Between roots
welled up the blood that makes its way to men,
and it looked as heavy as porphyry in the dark.
There was nothing else red.

There were crags there
and insubstantial forests. Bridges over vacuity
and that large, gray, blind pool
which hung above its distant bottom
like rainy skies over a landscape.
And between meadows, gentle and full of forbearance,
appeared the pale strip of the only path,
laid out like a long bleaching ground.

And along that one path they came.

In front, the slender man in the blue cloak,
who, mute and impatient, gazed ahead of him.
Without chewing, his paces gobbled up the path
in big bites; his hands hung,
heavy and closed, out of the fall of his drapery
and had no recollection of the light lyre
that had grown into his left arm
like rose tendrils into the branch of the olive tree.
And his senses were as if sundered:
while his gaze ran out before him like a dog,
turned around, came back, and time and again stood
far off, waiting at the next bend—
his hearing remained behind like a scent.
At times he felt as if it reached
all the way to where those other two were walking,
they who were to follow along that whole ascent.
At other times it was only the echo of his climbing,

und seines Mantels Wind was hinter ihm war.
Er aber sagte sich, sie kämen doch;
sagte es laut und hörte sich verhallen.
Sie kämen doch, nur wärens zwei
die furchtbar leise gingen. Dürfte er
sich einmal wenden (wäre das Zurückschaun
nicht die Zersetzung dieses ganzen Werkes,
das erst vollbracht wird), müßte er sie sehen,
die beiden Leisen, die ihm schweigend nachgehn:

Den Gott des Ganges und der weiten Botschaft,
die Reisehaube über hellen Augen,
den schlanken Stab hertragend vor dem Leibe
und flügelschlagend an den Fußgelenken;
und seiner linken Hand gegeben: *sie.*

Die So-geliebte, daß aus einer Leier
mehr Klage kam als je aus Klagefrauen;
daß eine Welt aus Klage ward, in der
alles noch einmal da war: Wald und Tal
und Weg und Ortschaft, Feld und Fluß und Tier;
und daß um diese Klage-Welt, ganz so
wie um die andre Erde, eine Sonne
und ein gestirnter stiller Himmel ging,
ein Klage-Himmel mit entstellten Sternen—:
Diese So-geliebte.

Sie aber ging an jenes Gottes Hand,
den Schritt beschränkt von langen Leichenbändern,
unsicher, sanft und ohne Ungeduld.
Sie war in sich, wie Eine hoher Hoffnung,
und dachte nicht des Mannes, der voranging,
und nicht des Weges, der ins Leben aufstieg.
Sie war in sich. Und ihr Gestorbensein
erfüllte sie wie Fülle.
Wie eine Frucht von Süßigkeit und Dunkel,
so war sie voll von ihrem großen Tode,
der also neu war, daß sie nichts begriff.

Sie war in einem neuen Mädchentum
und unberührbar; ihr Geschlecht war zu
wie eine junge Blume gegen Abend,
und ihre Hände waren der Vermählung

and the breeze from his cloak, that was behind him.
But he told himself they were really coming;
he said it out loud and heard his voice die away.
Yes, really coming, but they were two
who walked terribly quietly. Were he permitted
to turn around just once (were looking back
not the ruin of this entire task,
only now being accomplished), he couldn't help seeing them,
the two quiet ones following him in silence:

the god of errands and of far-borne messages,
his traveling hat over his bright eyes,
carrying his narrow wand in front of his body,
wings beating against his ankles;
and plighted to his left hand: *her*,

the woman so beloved that from a lyre
more lament issued than ever from professional mourners;
that a world was formed from lament, a world in which
everything could be found again: forest and valley
and road and hamlet, field and river and beast;
and that around this world of lament, just as
around the other earth, a sun
and a calm, starry sky circled,
a sky of lament with disfigured stars—
this woman so beloved.

But she walked holding that god's hand,
her steps impeded by long winding sheets,
uncertain, gentle, and without impatience.
She was contained in herself, like a woman with lofty expectancy,
with no thought of the man who was preceding,
or of the path that ascended into life.
She was within herself. And her state of having died
filled her like abundance.
Like a fruit of sweetness and darkness,
so she was filled with her great death,
which was so new that she understood nothing.

She was in a new virginity
and untouchable; her sex was shut
like a young flower toward evening,
and her hands were so disaccustomed

so sehr entwöhnt, daß selbst des leichten Gottes
unendlich leise, leitende Berührung
sie kränkte wie zu sehr Vertraulichkeit.

Sie war schon nicht mehr diese blonde Frau,
die in des Dichters Liedern manchmal anklang,
nicht mehr des breiten Bettes Duft und Eiland
und jenes Mannes Eigentum nicht mehr.

Sie war schon aufgelöst wie langes Haar
und hingegeben wie gefallner Regen
und ausgeteilt wie hundertfacher Vorrat.

Sie war schon Wurzel.

Und als plötzlich jäh
der Gott sie anhielt und mit Schmerz im Ausruf
die Worte sprach: Er hat sich umgewendet—,
begriff sie nichts und sagte leise: Wer?

Fern aber, dunkel vor dem klaren Ausgang,
stand irgend jemand, dessen Angesicht
nicht zu erkennen war. Er stand und sah,
wie auf dem Streifen eines Wiesenpfades
mit trauervollem Blick der Gott der Botschaft
sich schweigend wandte, der Gestalt zu folgen,
die schon zurückging dieses selben Weges,
den Schritt beschränkt von langen Leichenbändern,
unsicher, sanft und ohne Ungeduld.

68. Alkestis

Da plötzlich war der Bote unter ihnen,
hineingeworfen in das Überkochen
des Hochzeitsmahles wie ein neuer Zusatz.
Sie fühlten nicht, die Trinkenden, des Gottes
heimlichen Eintritt, welcher seine Gottheit
so an sich hielt wie einen nassen Mantel
und ihrer einer schien, der oder jener,
wie er so durchging. Aber plötzlich sah
mitten im Sprechen einer von den Gästen
den jungen Hausherrn oben an dem Tische

to marital relations that even the light god's
infinitely soft touch as he led her
offended her like too great intimacy.

By now she was no longer that blonde woman
so often mentioned in the poet's songs,
no longer the fragrance and island of their wide bed,
and no longer that man's property.

By now she was unbound, like long hair,
and dedicated, like fallen rain,
and parceled out, like hundredfold provisions.

She was already root.

And when suddenly, abruptly,
the god restrained her and, sorrow in his exclamation,
spoke the words "He turned around"—
she understood nothing and said quietly, "Who?"

But in the distance, dark against the bright exit,
stood someone whose face
was unrecognizable. He stood and saw
how on the strip of meadow path
the god of envoys with a mournful gaze
turned back in silence to follow the figure
that was already returning down that same path,
her steps impeded by long winding sheets,
uncertain, gentle, and without impatience.

68. Alcestis

There was the messenger suddenly among them,
thrown into the boiling-over
of the wedding banquet like a new ingredient.
The people drinking didn't perceive the secret
entrance of the god, who held his godhood
as closely to him as a damp cloak
and seemed like one of them, just anybody,
as he passed through them that way. But suddenly,
while speaking, one of the guests saw
the young host at the head of the table

wie in die Höh gerissen, nicht mehr liegend,
und überall und mit dem ganzen Wesen
ein Fremdes spiegelnd, das ihn furchtbar ansprach.
Und gleich darauf, als klärte sich die Mischung,
war Stille; nur mit einem Satz am Boden
von trübem Lärm und einem Niederschlag
fallenden Lallens, schon verdorben riechend
nach dumpfem umgestandenen Gelächter.
Und da erkannten sie den schlanken Gott,
und wie er dastand, innerlich voll Sendung
und unerbittlich,—wußten sie es beinah.
Und doch, als es gesagt war, war es mehr
als alles Wissen, gar nicht zu begreifen.
Admet muß sterben. Wann? In dieser Stunde.

Der aber brach die Schale seines Schreckens
in Stücken ab und streckte seine Hände
heraus aus ihr, um mit dem Gott zu handeln.
Um Jahre, um ein einzig Jahr noch Jugend,
um Monate, um Wochen, um paar Tage,
ach, Tage nicht, um Nächte, nur um Eine,
um Eine Nacht, um diese nur: um die.
Der Gott verneinte, und da schrie er auf
und schrie's hinaus und hielt es nicht und schrie
wie seine Mutter aufschrie beim Gebären.

Und die trat zu ihm, eine alte Frau,
und auch der Vater kam, der alte Vater,
und beide standen, alt, veraltet, ratlos,
beim Schreienden, der plötzlich, wie noch nie
so nah, sie ansah, abbrach, schluckte, sagte:
Vater,
liegt dir denn viel daran an diesem Rest,
an diesem Satz, der dich beim Schlingen hindert?
Geh, gieß ihn weg. Und du, du alte Frau,
Matrone,
was tust du denn noch hier: du hast geboren.
Und beide hielt er sie wie Opfertiere
in Einem Griff. Auf einmal ließ er los
und stieß die Alten fort, voll Einfall, strahlend
und atemholend, rufend: Kreon, Kreon!
Und nichts als das; und nichts als diesen Namen.

as if torn upward, no longer reclining,
and everywhere and with his whole being
reflecting something strange that made a terrible claim upon him.
And immediately afterward, as if the mixture was being clarified,
there was silence; but with a sediment at the bottom
of dismal noise and a deposit
of diminishing babble, already with a rotting smell
of muffled laughter that had died like an animal.
And then they recognized the slender god,
and as he stood there, inwardly filled with his mission
and inexorable—they practically knew what was afoot.
Yet, when it was spoken, it exceeded
all knowledge, it was totally incomprehensible.
Admetus must die. When? Within the hour.

But he broke the bowl of his terror
to bits and extended his hands
out of it, in order to bargain with the god.
For a few years, for just one more year of youth,
for months, for weeks, for a couple of days,
ah! not days, for nights, for just one,
for one night, just for this one: for it!
The god refused, and then he cried out
and yelled it out and couldn't bear it and screamed
as his mother had screamed when giving birth to him.

And she came over to him, an elderly woman,
and his father came, too, his elderly father,
and both stood, old, antiquated, helpless,
beside the shouting man, who suddenly, as if never before
so closely, looked at them, broke off, sobbed, said:
"Father,
is this remnant of life really very important to you,
this sediment which hinders you when you swallow?
Go, pour it out. And you, you old woman,
matron,
what are you doing still here? You have given birth."
And he held the two like sacrificial animals
in a single grasp. All at once he released
the old couple, shoving them away, full of inspiration, beaming
and catching his breath, calling: "Creon, Creon!"
And nothing else; and nothing but that name.

Aber in seinem Antlitz stand das Andere,
das er nicht sagte, namenlos erwartend,
wie ers dem jungen Freunde, dem Geliebten,
erglühend hinhielt übern wirren Tisch.
Die Alten (stand da), siehst du, sind kein Loskauf,
sie sind verbraucht und schlecht und beinah wertlos,
du aber, du, in deiner ganzen Schönheit—

Da aber sah er seinen Freund nicht mehr.
· Er blieb zurück, und das, was kam, war *sie*,
ein wenig kleiner fast als er sie kannte
und leicht und traurig in dem bleichen Brautkleid.
Die andern alle sind nur ihre Gasse,
durch die sie kommt und kommt—: (gleich wird sie da sein
in seinen Armen, die sich schmerzhaft auftun).

Doch wie er wartet, spricht sie; nicht zu ihm.
Sie spricht zum Gotte, und der Gott vernimmt sie,
und alle hörens gleichsam erst im Gotte:

Ersatz kann keiner für ihn sein. Ich *bins*.
Ich bin Ersatz. Denn keiner ist zu Ende
wie ich es bin. Was bleibt mir denn von dem
was ich hier war? Das *ists* ja, daß ich sterbe.
Hat sie dirs nicht gesagt, da sie dirs auftrug,
daß jenes Lager, das da drinnen wartet,
zur Unterwelt gehört? Ich nahm ja Abschied.
Abschied über Abschied.
Kein Sterbender nimmt mehr davon. Ich ging ja,
damit das Alles, unter Dem begraben
der jetzt mein Gatte ist, zergeht, sich auflöst—.
So führ mich hin: ich sterbe ja für ihn.

Und wie der Wind auf hoher See, der umspringt,
so trat der Gott fast wie zu einer Toten
und war auf einmal weit von ihrem Gatten,
dem er, versteckt in einem kleinen Zeichen,
die hundert Leben dieser Erde zuwarf.
Der stürzte taumelnd zu den beiden hin

But in his face stood that other thing,
which he didn't express, in unutterable expectancy,
as he enthusiastically extended it across the confused table
to his young friend, whom he loved.
"The old folks" (he stood there), "as you see, are no ransom,
they're used up, bad, and nearly worthless,
but you, you, in the fullness of your beauty—"

But then he no longer saw his friend.
He held back, and what came was *she*,
a little shorter, almost, than he remembered
and light and mournful in her pale wedding dress.
All the others are merely a thoroughfare for her,
through which she keeps on coming (at once she'll be there
in his arms, which open painfully).

But as he waits she speaks: not to him.
She addresses the god, and the god hears her,
and everyone hears it as if only through the god:

"No one can be a substitute for him. It's *me*.
I am the substitute. For no one else is as concluded
as I am. For what remains to me of that
which I was here? All this is *meant* for my death.
Weren't you told when given the assignment[4]
that the marriage bed waiting inside there
belongs to the underworld? I have said good-bye.
One good-bye after another.
No dying person says more of them. Yes, I came
so that all of this, buried beneath the man
who is now my husband, may crumble and dissolve. —
So take me away: for I shall die for him."

And like the wind on the open sea, which jumps around,
the god advanced, almost as if to a dead woman,
and all at once he was far from her husband,
to whom, concealed in a little sign,
he tossed the hundred lives of this earth.
Admetus, reeling, dashed after the two,

[4]In all likelihood, the *sie* doing the telling and giving in this line in the German refers to the underworld.

und griff nach ihnen wie im Traum. Sie gingen
schon auf den Eingang zu, in dem die Frauen
verweint sich drängten. Aber einmal sah
er noch des Mädchens Antlitz, das sich wandte
mit einem Lächeln, hell wie eine Hoffnung,
die beinah ein Versprechen war: erwachsen
zurückzukommen aus dem tiefen Tode
zu ihm, dem Lebenden—

Da schlug er jäh
die Hände vors Gesicht, wie er so kniete,
um nichts zu sehen mehr nach diesem Lächeln.

69. Geburt der Venus

An diesem Morgen nach der Nacht, die bang
vergangen war mit Rufen, Unruh, Aufruhr,—
brach alles Meer noch einmal auf und schrie.
Und als der Schrei sich langsam wieder schloß
und von der Himmel blassem Tag und Anfang
herabfiel in der stummen Fische Abgrund—:
gebar das Meer.

Von erster Sonne schimmerte der Haarschaum
der weiten Wogenscham, an deren Rand
das Mädchen aufstand, weiß, verwirrt und feucht.
So wie ein junges grünes Blatt sich rührt,
sich reckt und Eingerolltes langsam aufschlägt,
entfaltete ihr Leib sich in die Kühle
hinein und in den unberührten Frühwind.

Wie Monde stiegen klar die Kniee auf
und tauchten in der Schenkel Wolkenränder;
der Waden schmaler Schatten wich zurück,
die Füße spannten sich und wurden licht,
und die Gelenke lebten wie die Kehlen
von Trinkenden.

Und in dem Kelch des Beckens lag der Leib
wie eine junge Frucht in eines Kindes Hand.
In seines Nabels engem Becher war
das ganze Dunkel dieses hellen Lebens.

reaching out for them as if in a dream. They were already
proceeding toward the entrance, where the women
crowded with tear-stained eyes. But, once again,
he saw the girl's face, turning back
with a smile that was bright as a hope,
that was almost a promise: to return
as an adult from her deep death
to him, the living man—

Then he abruptly clapped
his hands to his face, as he knelt there,
to keep from seeing anything more after that smile.

69. Birth of Venus

On this morning after the night that had gone by
in fear with cries, unrest, turmoil—
the whole sea once more burst open and shouted.
And when the shout slowly closed again
and fell from the heavens' pale daylight and beginning,
down into the abyss of the mute fishes—
the sea gave birth.

In the first rays of sun glimmered the frothy hair
of the broad pudendum of waves, on the rim of which
the girl stood up, white, bewildered, and wet.
Just as a young green leaf stirs,
stretches, and slowly reveals what had been rolled up,
her body unfurled itself into the coolness
and into the untouched early breeze.

Like moons her knees arose brightly
and dove into the cloudy rims of her thighs;
her calves' narrow shadow receded,
her feet tautened and grew bright,
and her ankles were alive like the gullets
of people drinking.

And in the chalice of her pelvis her belly lay
like a young fruit in a child's hand.
In the narrow goblet of her navel was
all the darkness of that bright life.

Darunter hob sich licht die kleine Welle
und floß beständig über nach den Lenden,
wo dann und wann ein stilles Rieseln war.
Durchschienen aber und noch ohne Schatten,
wie ein Bestand von Birken im April,
warm, leer und unverborgen, lag die Scham.

Jetzt stand der Schultern rege Waage schon
im Gleichgewichte auf dem graden Körper,
der aus dem Becken wie ein Springbrunn aufstieg
und zögernd in den langen Armen abfiel
und rascher in dem vollen Fall des Haars.

Dann ging sehr langsam das Gesicht vorbei:
aus dem verkürzten Dunkel seiner Neigung
in klares, waagrechtes Erhobensein.
Und hinter ihm verschloß sich steil das Kinn.

Jetzt, da der Hals gestreckt war wie ein Strahl
und wie ein Blumenstiel, darin der Saft steigt,
streckten sich auch die Arme aus wie Hälse
von Schwänen, wenn sie nach dem Ufer suchen.

Dann kam in dieses Leibes dunkle Frühe
wie Morgenwind der erste Atemzug.
Im zartesten Geäst der Aderbäume
entstand ein Flüstern, und das Blut begann
zu rauschen über seinen tiefen Stellen.
Und dieser Wind wuchs an: nun warf er sich
mit allem Atem in die neuen Brüste
und füllte sie und drückte sich in sie,—
daß sie wie Segel, von der Ferne voll,
das leichte Mädchen nach dem Strande drängten.

So landete die Göttin.

Hinter ihr,
die rasch dahinschritt durch die jungen Ufer,
erhoben sich den ganzen Vormittag
die Blumen und die Halme, warm, verwirrt,
wie aus Umarmung. Und sie ging und lief.

Am Mittag aber, in der schwersten Stunde,
hob sich das Meer noch einmal auf und warf

Below, there brightly arose the small wave
that continuously overflowed toward her loins,
where there was an occasional quiet rippling.
But shone-through and still unshadowed,
like a stand of birches in April,
warm, empty, and unconcealed, lay her sex.

Now the active scale of her shoulders already stood
evenly balanced on her straight body,
which rose from her pelvis like a fountain
and fell away hesitatingly in her long arms
and more rapidly in the full tumbling of her hair.

Then her face went by very slowly:
out of the contracted darkness of its inclination
into a bright, horizontal raised position.
And behind it her chin closed itself steeply.

Now that her neck was extended like a ray
and like a flower's stem, in which the sap rises,
her arms, too, stretched out like necks
of swans when they search for the shore.

Then there came into the dark earliness of her body
the first drawing of breath, like a morning breeze.
In the tenderest ramification of her vein-trees
arose a whispering, and her blood began
to rumble over its deep places.
And this breeze increased: now it hurled itself
with all its breath into her new breasts
and filled them and pressed itself into them—
so that like sails full of the faraway they
urged the light girl to the shore.

Thus did the goddess reach the land.

Behind her,
as she quickly moved forward over the young shores,
there arose, all morning long,
the flowers and grasses, warm, confused,
as if from an embrace. And she went and ran.

But at noon, in the heaviest hour,
the sea rose once again and cast out

einen Delphin an jene selbe Stelle.
Tot, rot und offen.

70. Die Rosenschale

Zornige sahst du flackern, sahst zwei Knaben
zu einem Etwas sich zusammenballen,
das Haß war und sich auf der Erde wälzte
wie ein von Bienen überfallnes Tier;
Schauspieler, aufgetürmte Übertreiber,
rasende Pferde, die zusammenbrachen,
den Blick wegwerfend, bläkend das Gebiß
als schälte sich der Schädel aus dem Maule.

Nun aber weißt du, wie sich das vergißt:
denn vor dir steht die volle Rosenschale,
die unvergeßlich ist und angefüllt
mit jenem Äußersten von Sein und Neigen,
Hinhalten, Niemals-Gebenkönnen, Dastehn,
das unser sein mag: Äußerstes auch uns.

Lautloses Leben, Aufgehn ohne Ende,
Raum-brauchen ohne Raum von jenem Raum
zu nehmen, den die Dinge rings verringern,
fast nicht Umrissen-sein wie Ausgespartes
und lauter Inneres, viel seltsam Zartes
und Sich-bescheinendes—bis an den Rand:
ist irgend etwas uns bekannt wie dies?

Und dann wie dies: daß ein Gefühl entsteht,
weil Blütenblätter Blütenblätter rühren?
Und dies: daß eins sich aufschlägt wie ein Lid,
und drunter liegen lauter Augenlider,
geschlossene, als ob sie, zehnfach schlafend,
zu dämpfen hätten eines Innern Sehkraft.
Und dies vor allem: daß durch diese Blätter
das Licht hindurch muß. Aus den tausend Himmeln
filtern sie langsam jenen Tropfen Dunkel,
in dessen Feuerschein das wirre Bündel
der Staubgefäße sich erregt und aufbäumt.

Und die Bewegung in den Rosen, sieh:
Gebärden von so kleinem Ausschlagswinkel,

a dolphin at that same spot.
Dead, red, and open.

70. The Bowl of Roses

You've seen angry people flare up, seen two boys
clump together into a something
that was hate and rolled on the ground
like an animal attacked by bees;
playactors, going too far and exaggerating,
furious horses that have collapsed,
casting scornful glances, their teeth bared
as if their skull were being peeled out of their muzzle.

But now you know how to forget all that:
because before you stands the full bowl of roses,
which is unforgettable and filled
with that extreme of being and inclination,
holding oneself out, never being able to give, standing there,
which may be characteristic of us: an extreme even in us.

Soundless life, endless germination,
to need space without taking space
from that space which the things all round us diminish,
to have almost no contours, like a place left blank,
like something purely inward, like much that's oddly tender
and self-illuminating—to the very edge:
is anything as familiar to us as this?

Or then as this?—that an emotion arises
because petals touch petals?
Or this?—that one of them opens like an eyelid,
and beneath it lie nothing but eyelids,
closed ones, as if, asleep tenfold,
they had to curb the power of vision of something within.
Or this especially?—that light must make its way
through these petals. Out of the thousand skies
they slowly filter out that drop of darkness
in whose fiery glow the confused bundle
of stamens becomes excited and rears up.

And the movement in the roses, see:
gestures of so small an angle of deflection

daß sie unsichtbar blieben, liefen ihre
Strahlen nicht auseinander in das Weltall.

Sieh jene weiße, die sich selig aufschlug
und dasteht in den großen offnen Blättern
wie eine Venus aufrecht in der Muschel;
und die errötende, die wie verwirrt
nach einer kühlen sich hinüberwendet,
und wie die kühle fühllos sich zurückzieht,
und wie die kalte steht, in sich gehüllt,
unter den offenen, die alles abtun.
Und *was* sie abtun, wie das leicht und schwer,
wie es ein Mantel, eine Last, ein Flügel
und eine Maske sein kann, je nach dem,
und *wie* sie's abtun: wie vor dem Geliebten.

Was können sie nicht sein: war jene gelbe,
die hohl und offen daliegt, nicht die Schale
von einer Frucht, darin dasselbe Gelb,
gesammelter, orangeröter, Saft war?
Und wars für diese schon zu viel, das Aufgehn,
weil an der Luft ihr namenloses Rosa
den bittern Nachgeschmack des Lila annahm?
Und die batistene, ist sie kein Kleid,
in dem noch zart und atemwarm das Hemd steckt,
mit dem zugleich es abgeworfen wurde
im Morgenschatten an dem alten Waldbad?
Und diese hier, opalnes Porzellan,
zerbrechlich, eine flache Chinatasse
und angefüllt mit kleinen hellen Faltern,—
und jene da, die nichts enthält als sich.

Und sind nicht alle so, nur sich enthaltend,
wenn Sich-enthalten heißt: die Welt da draußen
und Wind und Regen und Geduld des Frühlings
und Schuld und Unruh und vermummtes Schicksal
und Dunkelheit der abendlichen Erde
bis auf der Wolken Wandel, Flucht und Anflug,
bis auf den vagen Einfluß ferner Sterne
in eine Hand voll Innres zu verwandeln.

Nun liegt es sorglos in den offnen Rosen.

that they would remain invisible if their beams
didn't diverge into the universe.

Look at that white one which has unfurled blissfully
and stands there with its big open petals
like a Venus upright on her seashell;
and the blushing one that, as if confused,
turns in the direction of a cool one,
and see how the cool one frigidly draws back
and how the cold one stands wrapped up in itself
among the open ones that strip themselves bare.
And *what* they strip off, how light or heavy it is—
it may be a cloak, a burden, a wing,
or a mask, depending on circumstances;
and *how* they strip it off; as if in their loved one's presence.

What can't they be?! Wasn't that yellow one,
which lies there hollow and open, the peel
of a fruit in which the same yellow,
more concentrated, more orange-red, was the juice?
And was its opening already too much for this one,
because from the air its inexpressible pink
took on the bitter aftertaste of lilac?
And that cambric one, isn't it a gown
in which the shift is still enclosed, tender and warm as breath,
the shift with which it was cast off at the same time
in the morning shade at the old bathing place in the woods?
And this one here, opaline porcelain,
fragile, a shallow china cup
and filled with little bright butterflies—
and that one, which contains only itself.

And aren't they all like that, containing only themselves;
if to contain oneself means to transform the world outside
and wind and rain and the patience of springtime
and guilt and unease and disguised destiny
and the darkness of the earth at evening
and even the alteration, flight, and approach of the clouds,
even the vague influence of distant stars,
into a handful of inwardness?

Now it lies, free of care, in the open roses.

71. Archaïscher Torso Apollos

Wir kannten nicht sein unerhörtes Haupt,
darin die Augenäpfel reiften. Aber
sein Torso glüht noch wie ein Kandelaber,
in dem sein Schauen, nur zurückgeschraubt,

sich hält und glänzt. Sonst könnte nicht der Bug
der Brust dich blenden, und im leisen Drehen
der Lenden könnte nicht ein Lächeln gehen
zu jener Mitte, die die Zeugung trug.

Sonst stünde dieser Stein entstellt und kurz
unter der Schultern durchsichtigem Sturz
und flimmerte nicht so wie Raubtierfelle;

und bräche nicht aus allen seinen Rändern
aus wie ein Stern: denn da ist keine Stelle,
die dich nicht sieht. Du mußt dein Leben ändern.

72. Leda

Als ihn der Gott in seiner Not betrat,
erschrak er fast, den Schwan so schön zu finden;
er ließ sich ganz verwirrt in ihm verschwinden.
Schon aber trug ihn sein Betrug zur Tat,

bevor er noch des unerprobten Seins
Gefühle prüfte. Und die Aufgetane
erkannte schon den Kommenden im Schwane
und wußte schon: er bat um Eins,

das sie, verwirrt in ihrem Widerstand,
nicht mehr verbergen konnte. Er kam nieder
und halsend durch die immer schwächre Hand

ließ sich der Gott in die Geliebte los.
Dann erst empfand er glücklich sein Gefieder
und wurde wirklich Schwan in ihrem Schooß.

71. Archaic Torso of Apollo

We never knew his astounding head,
in which the eyeballs matured. But
his torso still glows like a candelabrum
in which is gaze, though dimmed down,

persists and shines. Otherwise, the prow of his breast
couldn't dazzle you, and in the slight twist
of his loins a smile couldn't travel
to that midpoint which bore his genitals.

Otherwise, this stone would stand deformed and mutilated
beneath the translucent plunge of his shoulders,
and wouldn't shimmer so like the skins of beasts of prey;

and wouldn't break out of all its edges
like a star: for there's no place in it
that doesn't see you. You must change your life.

72. Leda

When the god in his distress entered it,
he was almost frightened to find the swan so beautiful;
completely confused, he let himself disappear into it.
But by now his deceit led him to the deed

even before he had tested the emotions
of an untried existence. And the woman, open to him,
already recognized the coming god in the swan
and already knew he was pleading for one thing

which she, confused in her resistance,
could no longer withhold. He descended
and, embracing her[5] between her increasingly weak hands,

the god released himself into the beloved.
Only then did he feel happy in his plumage,
becoming a swan truly in her lap.

---

[5]Or: "extending his neck."

73. Jeremia

Einmal war ich weich wie früher Weizen,
doch, du Rasender, du hast vermocht,
mir das hingehaltne Herz zu reizen,
daß es jetzt wie eines Löwen kocht.

Welchen Mund hast du mir zugemutet,
damals, da ich fast ein Knabe war:
eine Wunde wurde er: nun blutet
aus ihm Unglücksjahr um Unglücksjahr.

Täglich tönte ich von neuen Nöten,
die du, Unersättlicher, ersannst,
und sie konnten mir den Mund nicht töten;
sieh du zu, wie du ihn stillen kannst,

wenn, die wir zerstoßen und zerstören,
erst verloren sind und fernverlaufen
und vergangen sind in der Gefahr:
denn dann will ich in den Trümmerhaufen
endlich meine Stimme wiederhören,
die von Anfang an ein Heulen war.

74. Der aussätzige König

Da trat auf seiner Stirn der Aussatz aus
und stand auf einmal unter seiner Krone
als wär er König über allen Graus,
der in die Andern fuhr, die fassungsohne

hinstarrten nach dem furchtbaren Vollzug
an jenem, welcher, schmal wie ein Verschnürter,
erwartete, daß einer nach ihm schlug;
doch noch war keiner Manns genug:
als machte ihn nur immer unberührter
die neue Würde, die sich übertrug.

75. Der Stylit

Völker schlugen über ihm zusammen,
die er küren durfte und verdammen;

73. Jeremiah

Once I was soft as early wheat,
but you, furious one, were able
to stimulate the heart I held out to you
so that it now boils like a lion's.

What lips did you expect me to have
back then when I was nearly a boy?
They have become a wound: now
one year of misfortune after another bleeds from them.

Daily I resounded with new distresses,
which you insatiably thought up,
and they were unable to kill my lips;
it's now up to you to pacify them,

whenever those whom we crush and destroy
are finally lost, scattered far away,
and have perished in their peril:
for then in the heaps of ruins I want
to hear my voice again finally,
which from the very outset was a howl.

74. The Leper King

Then the leprosy broke out on his forehead
and stood there all at once below his crown
as if he were king over all horror,
which affected the others, who, losing their composure,

stared at the frightful progress of the disease
in the man who, slender as a person laced in,
expected someone to strike out at him;
but there was no one yet courageous enough:
as if he were merely made more and more untouchable
by that new dignity which became infectious.

75. The Stylite

Nations broke over him like waves,
nations he was permitted to choose or damn;

und erratend, daß er sich verlor,
klomm er aus dem Volksgeruch mit klammen
Händen einen Säulenschaft empor,

der noch immer stieg und nichts mehr hob,
und begann, allein auf seiner Fläche,
ganz von vorne seine eigne Schwäche
zu vergleichen mit des Herren Lob;

und da war kein Ende: er verglich;
und der Andre wurde immer größer.
Und die Hirten, Ackerbauer, Flößer
sahn ihn klein und außer sich

immer mit dem ganzen Himmel reden,
eingeregnet manchmal, manchmal licht;
und sein Heulen stürzte sich auf jeden,
so als heulte er ihm ins Gesicht.
Doch er sah seit Jahren nicht,

wie der Menge Drängen und Verlauf
unten unaufhörlich sich ergänzte,
und das Blanke an den Fürsten glänzte
lange nicht so hoch hinauf.

Aber wenn er oben, fast verdammt
und von ihrem Widerstand zerschunden,
einsam mit verzweifeltem Geschreie
schüttelte die täglichen Dämonen:
fielen langsam auf die erste Reihe
schwer und ungeschickt aus seinen Wunden
große Würmer in die offnen Kronen
und vermehrten sich im Samt.

76. Irre im Garten
Dijon

Noch schließt die aufgegebene Kartause
sich um den Hof, als würde etwas heil.
Auch die sie jetzt bewohnen, haben Pause
und nehmen nicht am Leben draußen teil.

Was irgend kommen konnte, das verlief.
Nun gehn sie gerne mit bekannten Wegen,

and, divining that he was going astray,
he climbed out of the people's smell with stiff
hands, up a column shaft

that kept on rising but no longer lifted anything,
and, alone on his flat platform, began
all over again to compare
his own weakness with the Lord's praise;

and then there was no end to it: he went on comparing;
and the Other One kept getting bigger.
And the shepherds, farmers, raftsmen
saw him as a small figure, beside himself,

always speaking to all the sky,
sometimes rain-soaked, sometimes shining;
and his howls swooped down on everyone
as if he were howling in the person's face.
But for years he hadn't seen

how the mob's crowding and dispersal
endlessly complemented each other down below,
and for some time the princes' shiny trim
hadn't gleamed that far upward.

But whenever, up there, nearly damned,
his skin all scraped by their resistance,
alone with desperate shouts
he shook off his daily demons,
there slowly fell onto the first row,
heavily and clumsily, from his wounds,
big worms, landing on the openwork crowns
and multiplying in the velvet.

76. Patients in the Madhouse Garden
Dijon

The secularized Carthusian monastery still encloses
the courtyard, as if something were becoming intact.
Those who now reside there also have time off
and don't participate in the life outside.

Whatever might have come has petered out.
Now they enjoy walking down familiar paths,

und trennen sich und kommen sich entgegen,
als ob sie kreisten, willig, primitiv.

Zwar manche pflegen dort die Frühlingsbeete,
demütig, dürftig, hingekniet;
aber sie haben, wenn es keiner sieht,
eine verheimlichte, verdrehte

Gebärde für das zarte frühe Gras,
ein prüfendes, verschüchtertes Liebkosen:
denn das ist freundlich, und das Rot der Rosen
wird vielleicht drohend sein und Übermaß

und wird vielleicht schon wieder übersteigen,
was ihre Seele wiederkennt und weiß.
Dies aber läßt sich noch verschweigen:
wie gut das Gras ist und wie leis.

77. Die Irren

Und sie schweigen, weil die Scheidewände
weggenommen sind aus ihrem Sinn,
und die Stunden, da man sie verstände,
heben an und gehen hin.

Nächtens oft, wenn sie ans Fenster treten:
plötzlich ist es alles gut.
Ihre Hände liegen im Konkreten,
und das Herz ist hoch und könnte beten,
und die Augen schauen ausgeruht

auf den unverhofften, oftentstellten
Garten im beruhigten Geviert,
der im Widerschein der fremden Welten
weiterwächst und niemals sich verliert.

78. Der Blinde
Paris

Sieh, er geht und unterbricht die Stadt,
die nicht ist auf seiner dunkeln Stelle,
wie ein dunkler Sprung durch eine helle
Tasse geht. Und wie auf einem Blatt

separating and meeting up again
as if in circles, willingly, primitively.

To be sure, many there tend the flowerbeds in spring,
humble, shabby, kneeling;
but when nobody is looking they make
a hidden, distorted

gesture at the tender early grass,
a groping, subdued caress:
because it's friendly, while the red of the roses
might be a threat and something excessive

and might once again go beyond
what their soul recognizes and knows.
But this still lets itself be discreetly concealed:
how good the grass is and how gentle!

77. The Insane

And they are silent because the partitions
have been removed from their mind,
and the hours when they might be understood
begin and go by.

Often at night, when they go to the window:
suddenly everything is good.
Their hands are on something concrete,
and their heart is uplifted and would be able to pray,
and their eyes, fully rested, look out

at the unexpected, frequently distorted
garden in the calmed quadrangle
that in the reflection of the strange worlds
continues to grow and never goes astray.

78. The Blind Man
Paris

Look: he's walking and interrupting the city,
which doesn't exist on the dark spot where he stands,
just as a dark crack traverses a bright
cup. And as if on a sheet of paper

ist auf ihm der Widerschein der Dinge
aufgemalt; er nimmt ihn nicht hinein.
Nur sein Fühlen rührt sich, so als finge
es die Welt in kleinen Wellen ein:

eine Stille, einen Widerstand—,
und dann scheint er wartend wen zu wählen:
hingegeben hebt er seine Hand,
festlich fast, wie um sich zu vermählen.

79. Eine Welke

Leicht, wie nach ihrem Tode
trägt sie die Handschuh, das Tuch.
Ein Duft aus ihrer Kommode
verdrängte den lieben Geruch,

an dem sie sich früher erkannte.
Jetzt fragte sie lange nicht, wer
sie sei (: eine ferne Verwandte),
und geht in Gedanken umher

und sorgt für ein ängstliches Zimmer,
das sie ordnet und schont,
weil es vielleicht noch immer
dasselbe Mädchen bewohnt.

80. Die Brandstätte

Gemieden von dem Frühherbstmorgen, der
mißtrauisch war, lag hinter den versengten
Hauslinden, die das Heidehaus beengten,
ein Neues, Leeres. Eine Stelle mehr,

auf welcher Kinder, von Gott weiß woher,
einander zuschrien und nach Fetzen haschten.
Doch alle wurden stille, sooft er,
der Sohn von hier, aus heißen, halbveraschten

Gebälken Kessel und verbogne Tröge
an einem langen Gabelaste zog,—

the reflection of objects on him
is laid on with paint; he doesn't absorb it.
Only his sense of touch is active, as if it perceived
the world in tiny waves:

a silence, a resistance—
and then he seems to choose somebody expectantly:
devotedly he lifts his hand,
almost festively, as if to be married.

79. A Faded Woman

Lightly, as if after her death,
she carries her glove, her shawl.
A fragrance from her commode
has supplanted the dear smell

by which she formerly recognized herself.
For a long time now she hasn't asked who
she is (a distant relative),
and she goes about lost in thought,

tending an anxious room,
arranging it and taking good care of it,
because perhaps it is still
lived in by the same girl.

80. The Scene of the Fire

Avoided by the early-fall morning, which
was distrustful, there lay behind the scorched
lime trees of the house, which crowded the house on the heath,
something new and empty. One more place

where children, coming from God knows where,
were yelling to one another and snatching at tatters.
But they all fell silent every time he,
the son of the household, drew kettles and bent vats

out of the hot, half-incinerated beams
with a long forked branch—

um dann mit einem Blick als ob er löge
die andern anzusehn, die er bewog

zu glauben, was an dieser Stelle stand.
Denn seit es nicht mehr war, schien es ihm so
seltsam: phantastischer als Pharao.
Und er war anders. Wie aus fernem Land.

81. Schlangen-Beschwörung

Wenn auf dem Markt, sich wiegend, der Beschwörer
die Kürbisflöte pfeift, die reizt und lullt,
so kann es sein, daß er sich einen Hörer
herüberlockt, der ganz aus dem Tumult

der Buden eintritt in den Kreis der Pfeife,
die will und will und will und die erreicht,
daß das Reptil in seinem Korb sich steife
und die das steife schmeichlerisch erweicht,

abwechselnd immer schwindelnder und blinder
mit dem, was schreckt und streckt, und dem, was löst—;
und dann genügt ein Blick: so hat der Inder
dir eine Fremde eingeflößt,

in der du stirbst. Es ist als überstürze
glühender Himmel dich. Es geht ein Sprung
durch dein Gesicht. Es legen sich Gewürze
auf deine nordische Erinnerung,

die dir nichts hilft. Dich feien keine Kräfte,
die Sonne gärt, das Fieber fällt und trifft;
von böser Freude steilen sich die Schäfte,
und in den Schlangen glänzt das Gift.

82. Papageien-Park
Jardin des Plantes, Paris

Unter türkischen Linden, die blühen, an Rasenrändern,
in leise von ihrem Heimweh geschaukelten Ständern
atmen die Ara und wissen von ihren Ländern,
die sich, auch wenn sie nicht hinsehn, nicht verändern.

and then, with a glance as if he were telling a lie,
looked at the others, whom he induced

to believe in what had stood on this spot.
For, since it no longer existed, it seemed to him so
odd: more fantastic than Pharaoh.
And *he* was different. As if from a faraway country.

81. Snake Charming

Whenever, in the marketplace, the swaying charmer
blows his gourd flute, which stimulates and lulls,
it may occur that he lures over to himself
some spectator, who entirely leaves the hubbub

of the fair booths and enters the circle of the flute,
which strongly exerts its will and succeeds
in making the reptile stiffen in its basket
and then in softening its stiffness with flattery,

alternating, ever more dizzily and blindly,
between that which frightens and stretches and that which loosens—
and then a look is enough: thus the Hindu has
infused a strangeness into you

in which you die. It's as if a fiery sky
fell down on you. A crack appears
across your face. Spices are added
to your Nordic memory,

which helps you not at all. No forces protect you,
the sun ferments, fever descends and strikes;
columns rise steeply in malicious joy,
and in the snakes the venom shines.

82. Parrot Park
Jardin des Plantes, Paris

Under blossoming Turkish lime trees at the edges of lawns,
in cages on stands gently rocked by their homesickness,
the macaws breathe and know about their native lands,
which don't change, even if they don't look in that direction.

Fremd im beschäftigten Grünen wie eine Parade,
zieren sie sich und fühlen sich selber zu schade,
und mit den kostbaren Schnäbeln aus Jaspis und Jade
kauen sie Graues, verschleudern es, finden es fade.

Unten klauben die duffen Tauben, was sie nicht mögen,
während sich oben die höhnischen Vögel verbeugen
zwischen den beiden fast leeren vergeudeten Trögen.

Aber dann wiegen sie wieder und schläfern und äugen,
spielen mit dunkelen Zungen, die gerne lögen,
zerstreut an den Fußfesselringen. Warten auf Zeugen.

83. Corrida
In memoriam Montez, 1830

Seit er, klein beinah, aus dem Toril
ausbrach, aufgescheuchten Augs und Ohrs,
und den Eigensinn des Picadors
und die Bänderhaken wie im Spiel

hinnahm, ist die stürmische Gestalt
angewachsen—sieh: zu welcher Masse,
aufgehäuft aus altem schwarzen Hasse,
und das Haupt zu einer Faust geballt,

nicht mehr spielend gegen irgendwen,
nein: die blutigen Nackenhaken hissend
hinter den gefällten Hörnern, wissend
und von Ewigkeit her gegen Den,

der in Gold und mauver Rosaseide
plötzlich umkehrt und, wie einen Schwarm
Bienen und als ob ers eben leide,
den Bestürzten unter seinem Arm

durchläßt,—während seine Blicke heiß
sich noch einmal heben, leichtgelenkt,
und als schlüge draußen jener Kreis
sich aus ihrem Glanz und Dunkel nieder
und aus jedem Schlagen seiner Lider,

ehe er gleichmütig, ungehässig,
an sich selbst gelehnt, gelassen, lässig

Strange as if on review in the busy greenery,
they preen themselves and feel they're too good for this,
and with their precious beaks of jasper and jade
they chew something gray, toss it away, find it insipid.

Below, dull-colored pigeons pick at something they don't like,
while, up above, the scornful birds incline themselves
between the two almost empty, squandered feeding trays.

But then they rock again, drowse, and give searching looks,
use their dark tongues, which would gladly tell lies, to play
distractedly with the rings attaching their feet. Waiting for witnesses.

83. Corrida [Bullfight]
In memoriam Montez, 1830

Ever since, almost small, he erupted
from the bullpen, with frightened eye and ear,
and tolerated the picador's obstinacy
and the banderillas, as if playfully,

his stormy figure
has grown (look: how massively!),
heaped up out of old, black hate,
and his head compacted into a fist,

no longer playing with any adversary,
no: hoisting the bloody hooks in his neck
behind his lowered horns, knowledgeable
and since all eternity opposed to the man

who, in gold and in mauve-pink silk,
suddenly turns and, as if it were a swarm
of bees and as if he could just barely tolerate it,
lets the bewildered bull pass through

under his arm—while his hot gaze
is raised once again, easily managed,
and as if that circle out there were precipitating
out of its light and shade
and every beat of its eyelids,

before he even-temperedly, free from hate,
self-supporting, calmly, nonchalantly

in die wiederhergerollte große
Woge über dem verlornen Stoße
seinen Degen beinah sanft versenkt.

84. Übung am Klavier

Der Sommer summt. Der Nachmittag macht müde;
sie atmete verwirrt ihr frisches Kleid
und legte in die triftige Etüde
die Ungeduld nach einer Wirklichkeit,

die kommen konnte: morgen, heute abend—,
die vielleicht da war, die man nur verbarg;
und vor den Fenstern, hoch und alles habend,
empfand sie plötzlich den verwöhnten Park.

Da brach sie ab; schaute hinaus, verschränkte
die Hände; wünschte sich ein langes Buch—
und schob auf einmal den Jasmingeruch
erzürnt zurück. Sie fand, daß er sie kränkte.

85. Das Rosen-Innere

Wo ist zu diesem Innen
ein Außen? Auf welches Weh
legt man solches Linnen ?
Welche Himmel spiegeln sich drinnen
in dem Binnensee
dieser offenen Rosen,
dieser sorglosen, sieh:
wie sie lose im Losen
liegen, als könnte nie
eine zitternde Hand sie verschütten.
Sie können sich selber kaum
halten; viele ließen
sich überfüllen und fließen
über von Innenraum
in die Tage, die immer
voller und voller sich schließen,

plunges his sword almost gently
into the great wave that has rolled back again
over the lost thrust.

84. Piano Practice

The summer hums. The afternoon makes one tired;
she was confusedly redolent of her fresh dress
and applied herself to the weighty etude
with impatience for some reality

which might come—tomorrow, that night—
which was perhaps already there and only concealed;
and at the windows, tall and all-containing,
she suddenly sensed the pampered park.

The she broke off, looked outside, clasped
her hands, wished she had a long book—
and all at once angrily repulsed
the smell of jasmine. She found it offensive to her.

85. The Heart of the Roses

Where, to match this inside,
is there an outside? To what wound
does one apply such linen?
What skies are reflected in there,
in the inland lake
of these open roses,
of these unworried ones? See
how loosely they lie
in looseness, as if no
trembling hand could ever spill them.
They can barely contain
themselves; many have let
themselves be filled too full and are flowing
over with inner space
into the days that are constantly
ending in greater and greater fullness,

bis der ganze Sommer ein Zimmer
wird, ein Zimmer in einem Traum.

86. Die Flamingos
Jardin des Plantes, Paris

In Spiegelbildern wie von Fragonard
ist doch von ihrem Weiß und ihrer Röte
nicht mehr gegeben, als dir einer böte,
wenn er von seiner Freundin sagt: sie war

noch sanft von Schlaf. Denn steigen sie ins Grüne
und stehn, auf rosa Stielen leicht gedreht,
beisammen, blühend, wie in einem Beet,
verführen sie verführender als Phryne

sich selber; bis sie ihres Auges Bleiche
hinhalsend bergen in der eignen Weiche,
in welcher Schwarz und Fruchtrot sich versteckt.

Auf einmal kreischt ein Neid durch die Volière;
sie aber haben sich erstaunt gestreckt
und schreiten einzeln ins Imaginäre.

87. Die Entführung

Oft war sie als Kind ihren Dienerinnen
entwichen, um die Nacht und den Wind
(weil sie drinnen so anders sind)
draußen zu sehn an ihrem Beginnen;

doch keine Sturmnacht hatte gewiß
den riesigen Park so in Stücke gerissen,
wie ihn jetzt ihr Gewissen zerriß,

da er sie nahm von der seidenen Leiter
und sie weitertrug, weiter, weiter . . . :

bis der Wagen alles war.

until the whole summer becomes
a room, a room within a dream.

86. The Flamingos
Jardin des Plantes, Paris

In reflections à la Fragonard,
nevertheless no more of their white
and ruddiness is shown than someone would offer you
if he said of his mistress that she was

still gentle with sleep. For when they step into the greenery
and stand, lightly turned on pink stems,
together, blossoming, as if in a flowerbed,
they seduce themselves more seductively

than Phryne; until, folding their necks, they hide
the pallor of their eyes in their own flanks,[6]
where black and fruit-red lie concealed.

All at once some envy screeches through the aviary;
but they have stretched themselves in astonishment
and now stride, one by one, into the imaginary.

87. The Elopement

Often as a child she had eluded
her servant women, in order to see the night and wind
(because they're so different indoors)
outside and at their outset;

but surely no stormy night had ever
torn the gigantic park to bits the way
her conscience was now rending her,

as he took her from the silken ladder
and bore her away, farther and farther. . . :

until the carriage was the whole world.

---

[6]Or: "their own softness."

Und sie roch ihn, den schwarzen Wagen,
um den verhalten das Jagen stand
und die Gefahr.
Und sie fand ihn mit Kaltem ausgeschlagen;
und das Schwarze und Kalte war auch in ihr.
Sie kroch in ihren Mantelkragen
und befühlte ihr Haar, als bliebe es hier,
und hörte fremd einen Fremden sagen:
Ichbinbeidir.

88. Mohammeds Berufung

Da aber als in sein Versteck der Hohe,
sofort Erkennbare: der Engel, trat,
aufrecht, der lautere und lichterlohe:
da tat er allen Anspruch ab und bat

bleiben zu dürfen der von seinen Reisen
innen verwirrte Kaufmann, der er war;
er hatte nie gelesen – und nun gar
ein *solches* Wort, zu viel für einen Weisen.

Der Engel aber, herrisch, wies und wies
ihm, was geschrieben stand auf seinem Blatte,
und gab nicht nach und wollte wieder: *Lies.*

Da las er: so, daß sich der Engel bog.
Und war schon einer, der gelesen *hatte*
und konnte und gehorchte und vollzog.

89. [Requiem] Für eine Freundin

Ich habe Tote, und ich ließ sie hin
und war erstaunt, sie so getrost zu sehn,
so rasch zuhaus im Totsein, so gerecht,
so anders als ihr Ruf. Nur du, du kehrst
zurück; du streifst mich, du gehst um, du willst
an etwas stoßen, daß es klingt von dir
und dich verrät. O nimm mir nicht, was ich
langsam erlern. Ich habe recht; du irrst

And she smelled it, that black carriage,
around which the subdued pursuit hovered,
and the peril.
And she found that it was lined with cold material;
and the blackness and coldness were in her as well.
She crept into her mantle collar
and fingered her hair, as if it were to remain behind,
and in estrangement heard a stranger say:
"Iamwithyou."

88. The Calling of Mohammed

But when there stepped into his hiding place
the tall, immediately recognizable one—the angel—
erect, pure, and ablaze:
then he laid aside all pretensions and pleaded

to be allowed to remain what he was,
a merchant inwardly confused by his travels;
he had never read—and now, indeed,
a world like *that*, too much even for a wise man!

But the angel imperiously kept on showing
him what was written on his sheet,
and made no concession, but kept insisting: "Read!"

Then he read: in such a way that the angel bowed.
And he was already one who *had* read
and had ability and obeyed and accomplished.

89. [Requiem] For a Woman Friend

I have my dead, and I have let them go
and have been amazed to find them of such good cheer,
so quickly at home in death, so righteous,
so different from their reputation. Only you, you come
back; you graze me, you go about, you want
to jostle something so you can make it emit a sound
and betray your presence. Oh, don't take from me what I
have slowly been learning! I'm in the right; you're wrong

wenn du gerührt zu irgend einem Ding
ein Heimweh hast. Wir wandeln dieses um;
es ist nicht hier, wir spiegeln es herein
aus unserm Sein, sobald wir es erkennen.
　　Ich glaubte dich viel weiter. Mich verwirrts,
daß *du* gerade irrst und kommst, die mehr
verwandelt hat als irgend eine Frau.
Daß wir erschraken, da du starbst, nein, daß
dein starker Tod uns dunkel unterbrach,
das Bisdahin abreißend vom Seither:
das geht uns an; das einzuordnen wird
die Arbeit sein, die wir mit allem tun.
Doch daß du selbst erschrakst und auch noch jetzt
den Schrecken hast, wo Schrecken nicht mehr gilt;
daß du von deiner Ewigkeit ein Stück
verlierst und hier hereintrittst, Freundin, hier,
wo alles noch nicht *ist;* daß du zerstreut,
zum ersten Mal im All zerstreut und halb,
den Aufgang der unendlichen Naturen
nicht so ergriffst wie hier ein jedes Ding;
daß aus dem Kreislauf, der dich schon empfing,
die stumme Schwerkraft irgend einer Unruh
dich niederzieht zur abgezählten Zeit—:
dies weckt mich nachts oft wie ein Dieb, der einbricht.
Und dürft ich sagen, daß du nur geruhst,
daß du aus Großmut kommst, aus Überfülle,
weil du so sicher bist, so in dir selbst,
daß du herumgehst wie ein Kind, nicht bange
vor Örtern, wo man einem etwas tut—:
doch nein: du bittest. Dieses geht mir so
bis ins Gebein und querrt wie eine Säge.
Ein Vorwurf, den du trügest als Gespenst,
nachtrügest mir, wenn ich mich nachts zurückzieh
in meine Lunge, in die Eingeweide,
in meines Herzens letzte ärmste Kammer,—
ein solcher Vorwurf wäre nicht so grausam,
wie dieses Bitten ist. Was bittest du?
　　Sag, soll ich reisen? Hast du irgendwo
ein Ding zurückgelassen, das sich quält
und das dir nachwill? Soll ich in ein Land,

if you're stirred and feel nostalgia for
any thing. We transform it;
it isn't here, we cast its reflection
out of our own being as soon as we recognize it.
   I thought you had made much more progress. It confuses me
that you of all people wander and come, you that
have transformed more things than any other woman.
If we were frightened when you died—no: if
your strong death obscurely interrupted our life,
rending the up-to-then from the since-then—
that's our concern; to put it all in its place will be
the task we perform in everything we undertake.
But the fact that you yourself were frightened and even now
still feel the fear, when fear's no longer valid;
that you are losing a piece of your
eternity and entering here, my friend, here
where everything does not yet exist; that you distractedly,
scattered for the first time in the universe, and incomplete,
haven't understood the germination
of infinite natures as you understood each thing here;
that out of the cycle which has already received you
the mute gravitation of some restlessness
draws you downward into calculated time:
this often wakes me at night like a burglar breaking in.
And I wish I could say that you're merely condescending,
that you're coming out of generosity, out of abundance,
because you're so confident, so self-contained,
that you go about like a child, unafraid
of places where people do others harm!—
But no: you're pleading. This cuts so
deeply into my marrow and buzzes like a saw.
A reproach which you might be harboring as a ghost,
which you might hold against me when I withdraw at night
into my lungs, into my bowels,
into the last, poorest chamber of my heart—
such a reproach wouldn't be as cruel
as this pleading is. What do you ask for?
   Tell me, am I to travel? Have you left a thing
behind somewhere which is tormenting itself
and wants to follow you? Should I go to a country

das du nicht sahst, obwohl es dir verwandt
war wie die andre Hälfte deiner Sinne?
    Ich will auf seinen Flüssen fahren, will
an Land gehn und nach alten Sitten fragen,
will mit den Frauen in den Türen sprechen
und zusehn, wenn sie ihre Kinder rufen.
Ich will mir merken, wie sie dort die Landschaft
umnehmen draußen bei der alten Arbeit
der Wiesen und der Felder; will begehren,
vor ihren König hingeführt zu sein,
und will die Priester durch Bestechung reizen,
daß sie mich legen vor das stärkste Standbild
und fortgehn und die Tempeltore schließen.
Dann aber will ich, wenn ich vieles weiß,
einfach die Tiere anschaun, daß ein Etwas
von ihrer Wendung mir in die Gelenke
herübergleitet; will ein kurzes Dasein
in ihren Augen haben, die mich halten
und langsam lassen, ruhig, ohne Urteil.
Ich will mir von den Gärtnern viele Blumen
hersagen lassen, daß ich in den Scherben
der schönen Eigennamen einen Rest
herüberbringe von den hundert Düften.
Und Früchte will ich kaufen, Früchte, drin
das Land noch einmal ist, bis an den Himmel.
    Denn Das verstandest du: die vollen Früchte.
Die legtest du auf Schalen vor dich hin
und wogst mit Farben ihre Schwere auf.
Und so wie Früchte sahst du auch die Fraun
und sahst die Kinder so, von innen her
getrieben in die Formen ihres Daseins.
Und sahst dich selbst zuletzt wie eine Frucht,
nahmst dich heraus aus deinen Kleidern, trugst
dich vor den Spiegel, ließest dich hinein
bis auf dein Schauen; das blieb groß davor
und sagte nicht: das bin ich; nein: dies ist.
So ohne Neugier war zuletzt dein Schaun
und so besitzlos, von so wahrer Armut,
daß es dich selbst nicht mehr begehrte: heilig.
    So will ich dich behalten, wie du dich
hinstelltest in den Spiegel, tief hinein

you never saw, though it was related to you
like the other half of your senses?
    I'll journey down its rivers, I'll
go ashore and inquire into old customs,
I'll speak with the women in their doorways
and watch them calling their children.
I'll observe how they don the landscape there
when outdoors at their old tasks
in the meadows and fields; I'll desire
to be led into their king's presence
and I'll incite the priests by bribery
to place me before their mightiest idol
while they depart and shut the temple gates.
But then, when I know a lot, I'll
simply observe the animals, so that something
of their ways slips over
into my joints; I'll enjoy a brief existence
in their eyes, which will retain me
and slowly release me, calmly, forming no judgment.
I'll have the gardeners tell me the names
of many flowers, so that in the flowerpots
of their lovely appellations I can bring back here
a remnant of their hundred fragrances.
And I'll buy fruit, fruit in which
the land is still contained, up to the sky.

    Because you did understand *that*: ripe fruits.
You placed them in bowls in front of you
and weighed their heaviness with paints.
And just like fruit you saw women, too,
and saw children that way, cast from within
into the molds of their existence.
And you saw yourself, lastly, as a fruit;
you peeled yourself out of your clothing, stepped
in front of the mirror, and entered it completely
except for your gaze; that remained, mightily, outside
and said, not "That's me," but: "This exists."
At the end your gaze was so devoid of curiosity
and of possession, it was of such genuine poverty,
that it no longer desired you yourself: it was holy.

    That's how I want to retain you, the way you
entered the mirror, deep inside it

und fort von allem. Warum kommst du anders?
Was widerrufst du dich? Was willst du mir
einreden, daß in jenen Bernsteinkugeln
um deinen Hals noch etwas Schwere war
von jener Schwere, wie sie nie im Jenseits
beruhigter Bilder ist; was zeigst du mir
in deiner Haltung eine böse Ahnung;
was heißt dich die Konturen deines Leibes
auslegen wie die Linien einer Hand,
daß ich sie nicht mehr sehn kann ohne Schicksal?
    Komm her ins Kerzenlicht. Ich bin nicht bang,
die Toten anzuschauen. Wenn sie kommen,
so haben sie ein Recht, in unserm Blick
sich aufzuhalten, wie die andern Dinge.
    Komm her; wir wollen eine Weile still sein.
Sieh diese Rose an auf meinem Schreibtisch;
ist nicht das Licht um sie genau so zaghaft
wie über dir: sie dürfte auch nicht hier sein.
Im Garten draußen, unvermischt mit mir,
hätte sie bleiben müssen oder hingehn,—
nun währt sie so: was ist ihr mein Bewußtsein?

    Erschrick nicht, wenn ich jetzt begreife, ach,
da steigt es in mir auf: ich kann nicht anders,
ich muß begreifen, und wenn ich dran stürbe.
Begreifen, daß du hier bist. Ich begreife.
Ganz wie ein Blinder rings ein Ding begreift,
fühl ich dein Los und weiß ihm keinen Namen.
Laß uns zusammen klagen, daß dich einer
aus deinem Spiegel nahm. Kannst du noch weinen?
Du kannst nicht. Deiner Tränen Kraft und Andrang
hast du verwandelt in dein reifes Anschaun
und warst dabei, jeglichen Saft in dir
so umzusetzen in ein starkes Dasein,
das steigt und kreist, im Gleichgewicht und blindlings.
Da riß ein Zufall dich, dein letzter Zufall
riß dich zurück aus deinem fernsten Fortschritt
in eine Welt zurück, wo Säfte *wollen*.
Riß dich nicht ganz; riß nur ein Stück zuerst,
doch als um dieses Stück von Tag zu Tag
die Wirklichkeit so zunahm, daß es schwer ward,

and away from all else. Why do you now come differently?
Why do you disavow yourself? Why do you want
to persuade me that in those amber beads
around your neck there was still something heavy,
of that heaviness which is never found in the Beyond
of calm pictures? Why do you show me
an evil foreboding in your bearing?
What makes you interpret the contours
of your body like the lines of a hand,
so I can no longer see them without sensing a destiny?
    Come here into the candlelight. I'm not afraid
to look at the dead. When they come
they have the right to linger
in our sight like all other things.
    Come here; we'll be still for a while.
Look at this rose on my desk;
isn't the light around it just as tremulous
as it is on you? The rose shouldn't be here, either.
It should have remained outside in the garden,
unmingled with me, or it should have perished—
now it lasts this way: what is my consciousness to it?

    Don't be afraid if I now understand; ah,
it now wells up in me: I can't help it,
I must understand even if it kills me.
Understand that you're here. I understand.
Just as a blind man understands the things around him,
I feel your fate but know no name for it.
Let's lament together because someone
has taken you out of your mirror. Can you still weep?
You can't. The strength and pressure of your tears
you have converted into your mature vision
and you were just about to transform all the sap
in you thus into that strong existence
which rises and circles, in equilibrium and blindly.
Then some chance tore you, your last-occurring chance
tore you back from your furthest progress,
back into a world where sap has *desires*.
Didn't tear you altogether; tore off only a bit at first,
but when around that bit, day by day,
so much reality grew that it became heavy,

da brauchtest du dich ganz: da gingst du hin
und brachst in Brocken dich aus dem Gesetz
mühsam heraus, weil du dich brauchtest. Da
trugst du dich ab und grubst aus deines Herzens
nachtwarmem Erdreich die noch grünen Samen,
daraus dein Tod aufkeimen sollte: deiner,
dein eigner Tod zu deinem eignen Leben.
Und aßest sie, die Körner deines Todes,
wie alle andern, aßest seine Körner,
und hattest Nachgeschmack in dir von Süße,
die du nicht meintest, hattest süße Lippen,
du: die schon innen in den Sinnen süß war.

    O laß uns klagen. Weißt du, wie dein Blut
aus einem Kreisen ohnegleichen zögernd
und ungern wiederkam, da du es abriefst?
Wie es verwirrt des Leibes kleinen Kreislauf
noch einmal aufnahm; wie es voller Mißtraun
und Staunen eintrat in den Mutterkuchen
und von dem weiten Rückweg plötzlich müd war.
Du triebst es an, du stießest es nach vorn,
du zerrtest es zur Feuerstelle, wie
man eine Herde Tiere zerrt zum Opfer;
und wolltest noch, es sollte dabei froh sein.
Und du erzwangst es schließlich: es war froh
und lief herbei und gab sich hin. Dir schien,
weil du gewohnt warst an die andern Maße,
es wäre nur für eine Weile; aber
nun warst du in der Zeit, und Zeit ist lang.
Und Zeit geht hin, und Zeit nimmt zu, und Zeit
ist wie ein Rückfall einer langen Krankheit.

    Wie war dein Leben kurz, wenn du's vergleichst
mit jenen Stunden, da du saßest und
die vielen Kräfte deiner vielen Zukunft
schweigend herabbogst zu dem neuen Kindkeim,
der wieder Schicksal war. O wehe Arbeit.
O Arbeit über alle Kraft. Du tatest
sie Tag für Tag, du schlepptest dich zu ihr
und zogst den schönen Einschlag aus dem Webstuhl
und brauchtest alle deine Fäden anders.
Und endlich hattest du noch Mut zum Fest.

you needed all of yourself: then you went out
and toilsomely broke yourself, in crumbs,
out of the law because you needed yourself. Then
you cleared yourself away and dug out of your heart's
nocturnally warm soil the still-green seeds
from which your death was to sprout: your own,
your death to match your own life.
And you ate them, those grains of your death;
like all the others, you ate its grains,
and felt a sweet aftertaste in you
that you hadn't expected, you had sweet lips,
you who were already sweet inwardly, in your senses.
   Oh, let's lament! Do you know how your blood
returned from its incomparable circulation
hesitantly and unwillingly when you called it back?
How in confusion it once again resumed that smaller circulation
in your body? How, full of mistrust
and amazement it entered your placenta
and suddenly grew weary from the long way back?
You drove it on, you pushed it forward,
you dragged it to the place of fire, just as
one drags a flock of animals to a sacrifice;
and, to boot, you wanted it to be glad about it.
And you finally compelled it: it was happy
and ran up to you and surrendered itself. You believed,
because you were accustomed to those other measurements,
that it was only for a while; but
now you were within time, and time is long.
And time goes by, and time increases, and time
is like a relapse in a long illness.
   How short your life was if you compare it
to those hours when you sat and
silently bent the many forces of your
rich future down to the new embryo,
which in turn was destiny! Oh, painful task!
Oh, a task beyond all our strength! You performed
it day after day, you hauled yourself to it
and pulled the beautiful weft out of the loom
and used all your threads differently.
And finally you still had courage to be festive.

Denn da's getan war, wolltest du belohnt sein,
wie Kinder, wenn sie bittersüßen Tee
getrunken haben, der vielleicht gesund macht.
So lohntest du dich: denn von jedem andern
warst du zu weit, auch jetzt noch; keiner hätte
ausdenken können, welcher Lohn dir wohltut.
Du wußtest es. Du saßest auf im Kindbett,
und vor dir stand ein Spiegel, der dir alles
ganz wiedergab. Nun war das alles *Du*
und ganz *davor,* und drinnen war nur Täuschung,
die schöne Täuschung jeder Frau, die gern
Schmuck umnimmt und das Haar kämmt und verändert.

So starbst du, wie die Frauen früher starben,
altmodisch starbst du in dem warmen Hause
den Tod der Wöchnerinnen, welche wieder
sich schließen wollen und es nicht mehr können,
weil jenes Dunkel, das sie mitgebaren,
noch einmal wiederkommt und drängt und eintritt.

Ob man nicht dennoch hätte Klagefrauen
auftreiben müssen? Weiber, welche weinen
für Geld, und die man so bezahlen kann,
daß sie die Nacht durch heulen, wenn es still wird.
Gebräuche her! wir haben nicht genug
Gebräuche. Alles geht und wird verredet.
So mußt du kommen, tot, und hier mit mir
Klagen nachholen. Hörst du, daß ich klage?
Ich möchte meine Stimme wie ein Tuch
hinwerfen über deines Todes Scherben
und zerrn an ihr, bis sie in Fetzen geht,
und alles, was ich sage, müßte so
zerlumpt in dieser Stimme gehn und frieren;
blieb es beim Klagen. Doch jetzt klag ich an:
den Einen nicht, der dich aus dir zurückzog,
(ich find ihn nicht heraus, er ist wie alle)
doch alle klag ich in ihm an: den Mann.
Wenn irgendwo ein Kindgewesensein
tief in mir aufsteigt, das ich noch nicht kenne,
vielleicht das reinste Kindsein meiner Kindheit:
ich wills nicht wissen. Einen Engel will
ich daraus bilden ohne hinzusehn

   Because when it was over you wanted to be rewarded,
like children when they've drunk
bittersweet tea which may restore their health.
In that way you rewarded yourself; for you were too far ahead
of anyone else, even then; no one could have
hit upon a reward beneficial to you.
You knew that. You sat up in your childbed,
and before you stood a mirror, which reflected everything
for you entirely. Now this everything was *you*
and completely *out front*, and inside there was only delusion,
the lovely delusion of every woman who likes
to put on jewelry and comb her hair and change its style.
   So you died as women formerly died;
in an old-fashioned way, in the warm house, you died
the death of women in labor who wish
to close themselves up again, but no longer can,
because that darkness to which they gave birth at the same time
returns once again and pushes and enters.

   Should we have hunted up some professional mourners
all the same? Females who weep
for money, and who can be paid so much
that they howl all night long, when it becomes quiet.
Give me the old customs! We don't have enough
old customs. Everything goes on until it's hackneyed.
And so you, a dead woman, must come and, here with me,
make up for those laments. Do you hear me lamenting?
I'd like to fling my voice like a sheet
over the shards of your death,
tugging it till it tears to shreds,
and every word I speak would have to go about
in tatters in that voice, and suffer from the cold;
if lamenting were all! But now I accuse:
not the one man who pulled you back out of yourself
(I can't detect him, he's like all the rest),
but I accuse all of them in him: the husband.
   If at some time a recollection of having been a child
wells up in me profoundly, one I'm not yet familiar with,
perhaps the purest child-existence of my childhood:
I won't want to know anything of it. I shall form
an angel out of it without looking

und will ihn werfen in die erste Reihe
schreiender Engel, welche Gott erinnern.
     Denn dieses Leiden dauert schon zu lang,
und keiner kanns; es ist zu schwer für uns,
das wirre Leiden von der falschen Liebe,
die, bauend auf Verjährung wie Gewohnheit,
ein Recht sich nennt und wuchert aus dem Unrecht.
Wo ist ein Mann, der Recht hat auf Besitz?
Wer kann besitzen, was sich selbst nicht hält,
was sich von Zeit zu Zeit nur selig auffängt
und wieder hinwirft wie ein Kind den Ball.
Sowenig wie der Feldherr eine Nike
festhalten kann am Vorderbug des Schiffes,
wenn das geheime Leichtsein ihrer Gottheit
sie plötzlich weghebt in den hellen Meerwind:
so wenig kann einer von uns die Frau
anrufen, die uns nicht mehr sieht und die
auf einem schmalen Streifen ihres Daseins
wie durch ein Wunder fortgeht, ohne Unfall:
er hätte denn Beruf und Lust zur Schuld.
     Denn *das* ist Schuld, wenn irgendeines Schuld ist:
die Freiheit eines Lieben nicht vermehren
um alle Freiheit, die man in sich aufbringt.
Wir haben, wo wir lieben, ja nur dies:
einander lassen; denn daß wir uns halten,
das fällt uns leicht und ist nicht erst zu lernen.

     Bist du noch da? In welcher Ecke bist du?—
Du hast so viel gewußt von alledem
und hast so viel gekonnt, da du so hingingst
für alles offen, wie ein Tag, der anbricht.
Die Frauen leiden: lieben heißt allein sein,
und Künstler ahnen manchmal in der Arbeit,
daß sie verwandeln müssen, wo sie lieben.
Beides begannst du; beides ist in Dem,
was jetzt ein Ruhm entstellt, der es dir fortnimmt.
Ach du warst weit von jedem Ruhm. Du warst
unscheinbar; hattest leise deine Schönheit
hineingenommen, wie man eine Fahne
einzieht am grauen Morgen eines Werktags,

and I'll fling him into the first row
of shouting angels who remind God about things.

   For this sorrow, by now, has lasted too long,
and no one can bear it; it's too heavy for us,
this chaotic sorrow due to that false love
which, relying on time-span and habit,
calls itself a right but proliferates from injustice.
Where is the man who has a right to property?
Who can own that which doesn't hold itself,
but merely, from time to time, catches itself happily
and tosses itself back again, as a child does with a ball?
Just as little as a general can keep a Victory
firmly fixed to the prow of his ship
when the mysterious lightness of her godhood
suddenly lifts her off into the bright sea wind:
so little can any of us call to
the woman who no longer sees us, but who
proceeds along the narrow path of her existence
as if by a miracle, without a mishap:
unless he had the vocation and desire for guilt.

   Because this *is* guilt, if anything is guilt:
not to increase the freedom of a loved one
with all the freedom one can muster up.
Yes, when we love, we have only this:
to let each other go; for, to hold onto each other
comes easily to us and doesn't have to be learned.

   Are you still there? In what corner are you?—
You knew so much about all this,
and you were so capable, when you went your way
open to everything, like a dawning day.
Women suffer: to love means to be alone,
and in their work artists sometimes foresee
that they must make transformations where they love.
You began both; both are contained in that
which is now disfigured by a fame that steals them from you.
Ah, you were far from all fame. You were
inconspicuous; you had gently drawn
your beauty in, just as a flag
is hauled down on the gray morning of a weekday,

und wolltest nichts, als eine lange Arbeit,—
die nicht getan ist: dennoch nicht getan.
    Wenn du noch da bist, wenn in diesem Dunkel
noch eine Stelle ist, an der dein Geist
empfindlich mitschwingt auf den flachen Schallwelln,
die eine Stimme, einsam in der Nacht,
aufregt in eines hohen Zimmers Strömung:
So hör mich: Hilf mir. Sieh, wir gleiten so,
nicht wissend wann, zurück aus unserm Fortschritt
in irgendwas, was wir nicht meinen; drin
wir uns verfangen wie in einem Traum
und drin wir sterben, ohne zu erwachen.
Keiner ist weiter. Jedem, der sein Blut
hinaufhob in ein Werk, das lange wird,
kann es geschehen, daß ers nicht mehr hochhält
und daß es geht nach seiner Schwere, wertlos.
Denn irgendwo ist eine alte Feindschaft
zwischen dem Leben und der großen Arbeit.
Daß ich sie einseh und sie sage: hilf mir.
    Komm nicht zurück. Wenn du's erträgst, so sei
tot bei den Toten. Tote sind beschäftigt.
Doch hilf mir so, daß es dich nicht zerstreut,
wie mir das Fernste manchmal hilft: in mir.

90. [Requiem] Für Wolf Graf von Kalckreuth

Sah ich dich wirklich nie ? Mir ist das Herz
so schwer von dir wie von zu schwerem Anfang,
den man hinausschiebt. Daß ich dich begänne
zu sagen, Toter der du bist; du gerne,
du leidenschaftlich Toter. War das so
erleichternd wie du meintest, oder war
das Nichtmehrleben doch noch weit vom Totsein?
Du wähntest, besser zu besitzen dort,
wo keiner Wert legt auf Besitz. Dir schien,
dort drüben wärst du innen in der Landschaft,
die wie ein Bild hier immer vor dir zuging,
und kämst von innen her in die Geliebte
und gingest hin durch alles, stark und schwingend.
O daß du nun die Täuschung nicht zu lang

and all you wanted was a lengthy task—
which remains undone: undone nevertheless.
   If you're still here, if in this darkness
there's still a spot where your spirit
is sensitively vibrating on the shallow sound waves
that a voice, lonely in the night,
excites in the current of a high-ceilinged room:
then hear me! Help me! See, we slip back in this way,
not knowing when, from our progress
into something we don't intend, and in which
we get entangled as in a dream,
and in which we die without awaking.
No one is past this. It can befall anyone
who has elevated his blood to a lengthy task
that he can no longer sustain it
and that it sinks by its own weight, becoming worthless.
For somewhere there's an ancient enmity
between life and the great task.
Help me to discern it and speak of it.
   Don't come back. If you can stand it, be
dead among the dead. Dead people are occupied.
But help me in such a way that it doesn't scatter your forces,
just as what is farthest away sometimes helps me: in me.

90. [Requiem] For Count Wolf von Kalckreuth

Did I really never see you? My heart
is as heavy with you as with a too heavy beginning
that one postpones. If only I could begin
to speak of you, dead man that you are, you willingly,
passionately dead man! Was it as
relieving as you thought, or was
no longer living still far from being dead?
You imagined you'd be more of a possessor there
where no one values possessions. It seemed to you
that in the beyond you'd be inside that landscape
which here always came before you like a picture,
and that, from within, you'd enter into that loved one
and would penetrate everything, strong and vibrant.
Oh, I hope you now won't hold that delusion too long

nachtrügest deinem knabenhaften Irrtum.
Daß du, gelöst in einer Strömung Wehmut
und hingerissen, halb nur bei Bewußtsein,
in der Bewegung um die fernen Sterne
die Freude fandest, die du von hier fort
verlegt hast in das Totsein deiner Träume.
Wie nahe warst du, Lieber, hier an ihr.
Wie war sie hier zuhaus, die, die du meintest,
die ernste Freude deiner strengen Sehnsucht.
Wenn du, enttäuscht von Glücklichsein und Unglück,
dich in dich wühltest und mit einer Einsicht
mühsam heraufkamst, unter dem Gewicht
beinah zerbrechend deines dunkeln Fundes:
da trugst du sie, sie, die du nicht erkannt hast,
die Freude trugst du, deines kleinen Heilands
Last trugst du durch dein Blut und holtest über.

Was hast du nicht gewartet, daß die Schwere
ganz unerträglich wird: da schlägt sie um
und ist so schwer, weil sie so echt ist. Siehst du,
dies war vielleicht dein nächster Augenblick;
er rückte sich vielleicht vor deiner Tür
den Kranz im Haar zurecht, da du sie zuwarfst.
O dieser Schlag, wie geht er durch das Weltall,
wenn irgendwo vom harten scharfen Zugwind
der Ungeduld ein Offenes ins Schloß fällt.
Wer kann beschwören, daß nicht in der Erde
ein Sprung sich hinzieht durch gesunde Samen;
wer hat erforscht, ob in gezähmten Tieren
nicht eine Lust zu töten geilig aufzuckt,
wenn dieser Ruck ein Blitzlicht in ihr Hirn wirft.
Wer kennt den Einfluß, der von unserm Handeln
hinüberspringt in eine nahe Spitze,
und wer begleitet ihn, wo alles leitet?
Daß du zerstört hast. Daß man dies von dir
wird sagen müssen bis in alle Zeiten.
Und wenn ein Held bevorsteht, der den Sinn,
den wir für das Gesicht der Dinge nehmen,

as a grudge against your boyish error!
I hope that, released into the melancholy of a current
and torn away, only half-consciously,
you may find in your motion around the distant stars
the joy that you removed from here
and transferred to the being-dead you dreamed about.
How close you were to that joy here, dear fellow!
How much at home it was here, the joy you expected,
the earnest joy of your austere longing!
Whenever, disappointed by being happy and by misfortune,
you burrowed into yourself and laboriously
reemerged with some insight, nearly broken
by the weight of your obscure discovery:
you were carrying it, though not recognizing it—
you were carrying that joy, you were carrying the burden
of your little savior through your blood and ferrying it over.

    Why didn't you wait for the heaviness
to become completely unbearable? At that point it veers
and is so heavy because it's so genuine. You see,
that might have befallen you at the very next moment;
perhaps that moment was straightening the wreath
in its hair outside your door when you slammed it.
    Oh, how that crash resounds through the universe
when somewhere, at a hard, sharp gust of the draft
of impatience, something open slams shut!
Who can swear that in the ground
a crack doesn't spread through healthy seeds?
Who has inquired whether in tamed animals
an urge to kill doesn't flare up lustfully
when that jolt casts a lightning flash into their brain?
Who knows the influence that leaps forth
from our doings onto a nearby point,
and who accompanies it where everything leads?[7]
    The fact that you have destroyed something. That people
will have to say that about you forever.
And if a hero appears who tears away
like a mask the meaning we take to be

---

[7]An eminent earlier translator translates *Spitze* as "terminal" and renders this last line as "who can conduct when everything's conductive?"

wie eine Maske abreißt und uns rasend
Gesichter aufdeckt, deren Augen längst
uns lautlos durch verstellte Löcher anschaun:
dies ist Gesicht und wird sich nicht verwandeln:
daß du zerstört hast. Blöcke lagen da,
und in der Luft um sie war schon der Rhythmus
von einem Bauwerk, kaum mehr zu verhalten;
du gingst herum und sahst nicht ihre Ordnung,
einer verdeckte dir den andern; jeder
schien dir zu wurzeln, wenn du im Vorbeigehn
an ihm versuchtest, ohne rechtes Zutraun,
daß du ihn hübest. Und du hobst sie alle
in der Verzweiflung, aber nur, um sie
zurückzuschleudern in den klaffen Steinbruch,
in den sie, ausgedehnt von deinem Herzen,
nicht mehr hineingehn. Hätte eine Frau
die leichte Hand gelegt auf dieses Zornes
noch zarten Anfang; wäre einer, der
beschäftigt war, im Innersten beschäftigt,
dir still begegnet, da du stumm hinausgingst,
die Tat zu tun—; ja hätte nur dein Weg
vorbeigeführt an einer wachen Werkstatt,
wo Männer hämmern, wo der Tag sich schlicht
verwirklicht; wär in deinem vollen Blick
nur so viel Raum gewesen, daß das Abbild
von einem Käfer, der sich müht, hineinging,
du hättest jäh bei einem hellen Einsehn
die Schrift gelesen, deren Zeichen du
seit deiner Kindheit langsam in dich eingrubst,
von Zeit zu Zeit versuchend, ob ein Satz
dabei sich bilde: ach, er schien dir sinnlos.
Ich weiß; ich weiß: du lagst davor und griffst
die Rillen ab, wie man auf einem Grabstein
die Inschrift abfühlt. Was dir irgend licht
zu brennen schien, das hieltest du als Leuchte
vor diese Zeile; doch die Flamme losch
eh du begriffst, vielleicht von deinem Atem,
vielleicht vom Zittern deiner Hand; vielleicht
auch ganz von selbst, wie Flammen manchmal ausgehn.
Du lasest's nie. Wir aber wagen nicht,
zu lesen durch den Schmerz und aus der Ferne.

the face of things, and who furiously
reveals to us faces whose eyes have long been
soundlessly watching us through disguised holes:
this is a face and it won't be changed:
the fact that you've been a destroyer. Building blocks lay there,
and in the air around them there was already the rhythm
of a construction, scarcely restrainable any longer;
you went around and failed to see their organization;
one block kept you from seeing the other; each of them
seemed to you to be rooted whenever, as you passed by,
you tried to pick it up
without being truly confident. And you lifted them all
in desperation, but only to
hurl them back into the gaping quarry,
into which, now expanded by your heart,
they no longer fit. Had a woman
laid her light hand on that anger's
still-gentle beginning; had someone who
was occupied, inwardly occupied,
met you silently when you set out mutely
to do the deed; yes, had your path only
led you past a lively workshop
where men hammer, where the day is
accomplished simply; had there been in your full gaze
only so much room that the image
of an industrious beetle could have entered,
you would have abruptly, with a clear realization,
read the writing whose characters you
had slowly been inscribing in yourself since your childhood,
trying to see every so often whether a sentence
might come out of it: alas, you thought it meaningless!
I know, I know: you lay in front of it and thumbed
the grooves, as one deciphers the inscription
on a tombstone by touch. Whatever you considered
to be burning brightly you held up as a light
in front of that line of writing; but the flame went out
before you understood it, perhaps from your breath,
perhaps from the trembling of your hand; perhaps
even, all by itself, as flames sometimes go out.
You never read it. But we don't dare
to read in pain and from a distance.

Nur den Gedichten sehn wir zu, die noch
über die Neigung deines Fühlens abwärts
die Worte tragen, die du wähltest. Nein,
nicht alle wähltest du; oft ward ein Anfang
dir auferlegt als Ganzes, den du nachsprachst
wie einen Auftrag. Und er schien dir traurig.
Ach hättest du ihn nie von dir gehört.
Dein Engel lautet jetzt noch und betont
denselben Wortlaut anders, und mir bricht
der Jubel aus bei seiner Art zu sagen,
der Jubel über dich: denn dies war dein:
Daß jedes Liebe wieder von dir abfiel,
daß du im Sehendwerden den Verzicht
erkannt hast und im Tode deinen Fortschritt.
Dieses war dein, du, Künstler; diese drei
offenen Formen. Sieh, hier ist der Ausguß
der ersten: Raum um dein Gefühl; und da
aus jener zweiten schlag ich dir das Anschaun
das nichts begehrt, des großen Künstlers Anschaun;
und in der dritten, die du selbst zu früh
zerbrochen hast, da kaum der erste Schuß
bebender Speise aus des Herzens Weißglut
hineinfuhr—, war ein Tod von guter Arbeit
vertieft gebildet, jener eigne Tod,
der uns so nötig hat, weil wir ihn leben,
und dem wir nirgends näher sind als hier.

Dies alles war dein Gut und deine Freundschaft;
du hast es oft geahnt; dann aber hat
das Hohle jener Formen dich geschreckt,
du griffst hinein und schöpftest Leere und
beklagtest dich.—O alter Fluch der Dichter,
die sich beklagen, wo sie sagen sollten,
die immer urteiln über ihr Gefühl
statt es zu bilden; die noch immer meinen,
was traurig ist in ihnen oder froh,
das wüßten sie und dürftens im Gedicht
bedauern oder rühmen. Wie die Kranken
gebrauchen sie die Sprache voller Wehleid,
um zu beschreiben, wo es ihnen wehtut,
statt hart sich in die Worte zu verwandeln,

We look only at the poems, which still,
over the inclination of your feelings downwards,
carry the words you chose. No,
you didn't choose them all; often a beginning was
imposed on you as a whole, a beginning you continued
like an assignment. And you found it sad.
O, I wish you had never heard it from yourself!
Your angel is still sounding and giving a different
stress to the same wording, and I break out
in rejoicing at his manner of reciting,
in rejoicing over you—for that was yours:
that everything dear fell away from you again,
that you recognized renunciation
in your gaining sight and your progress in your dying.
This was yours, you artist; these three
open molds. See, here is the casting
from the first one: space around your emotions. And here
from that second one I extract for you a gaze
free of desire, a great artist's gaze;
and in the third—which you yourself prematurely
shattered, while the first spurt
of bubbling metal from the white-hot glow of your heart
had scarcely entered it—was a death profoundly fashioned
from good work, that individual death of ours
which has such need of us because we live it,
and to which we're nowhere closer than we are here.

All this was your property and a friend to you;
you often had a presentiment of it; but then
the hollowness of those molds frightened you,
you reached into them and drew out emptiness, and
you were sorry for yourself. —Oh, that old curse of poets
who bewail themselves while they should be making statements,
who always sit in judgment over their emotions
instead of shaping them, who still always think
that whatever is sad in them or happy
is known to them and that they're allowed to regret it
or to praise it in a poem! Like sick people,
they use language full of whining
to describe where they feel an ache,
instead of severely converting themselves into words

wie sich der Steinmetz einer Kathedrale
verbissen umsetzt in des Steines Gleichmut.
    Dies war die Rettung. Hättest du nur *ein* Mal
gesehn, wie Schicksal in die Verse eingeht
und nicht zurückkommt, wie es drinnen Bild wird
und nichts als Bild, nicht anders als ein Ahnherr,
der dir im Rahmen, wenn du manchmal aufsiehst,
zu gleichen scheint und wieder nicht zu gleichen—:
du hättest ausgeharrt.

                    Doch dies ist kleinlich,
zu denken, was nicht war. Auch ist ein Schein
von Vorwurf im Vergleich, der dich nicht trifft.
Das, was geschieht, hat einen solchen Vorsprung
vor unserm Meinen, daß wirs niemals einholn
und nie erfahren, wie es wirklich aussah.

    Sei nicht beschämt, wenn dich die Toten streifen,
die andern Toten, welche bis ans Ende
aushielten. (Was will Ende sagen?) Tausche
den Blick mit ihnen, ruhig, wie es Brauch ist,
und fürchte nicht, daß unser Trauern dich
seltsam belädt, so daß du ihnen auffällst.
Die großen Worte aus den Zeiten, da
Geschehn noch sichtbar war, sind nicht für uns.
Wer spricht von Siegen? Überstehn ist alles.

91. Die Darstellung Mariae im Tempel

Um zu begreifen, wie sie damals war,
mußt du dich erst an eine Stelle rufen,
wo Säulen in dir wirken; wo du Stufen
nachfühlen kannst; wo Bogen voll Gefahr
den Abgrund eines Raumes überbrücken,
der in dir blieb, weil er aus solchen Stücken
getürmt war, daß du sie nicht mehr aus dir
ausheben kannst: du rissest dich denn ein.
Bist du so weit, ist alles in dir Stein,
Wand, Aufgang, Durchblick, Wölbung—, so probier
den großen Vorhang, den du vor dir hast,

as the stonemason of a cathedral
doggedly transforms himself into the stone's equanimity.
    That was your salvation. Had you seen
even *once* how destiny enters the verses
and never returns, how in the poem it becomes an image
and an image only, exactly like an ancestor
who, in the picture frame, if you sometimes look up,
seems now to resemble you, and another time not—
you would have endured to the end!

                                        But it's petty
to think about what never happened. Besides, there's a semblance
of reproach in the comparison that you don't deserve.
Whatever occurs had such a head start
over our thoughts that we never catch up with it
and never learn what it really looked like.
    Don't be ashamed when the dead brush against you,
the other dead who held out
to the very end. (What does "end" mean?) Exchange
glances with them, calmly, as is the custom,
and have no fear that our mourning will
burden you peculiarly, so that you attract their attention.
The proud words from those times when
occurrence was still visible are not for us.
Who speaks of victories? Survival is everything.

91. The Presentation of the Virgin in the Temple

To understand what she was like at the time
you must first summon yourself to a place
where columns operate on your mind; where you can
feel the presence of stairs; where arches full of peril
bridge the abyss of a space
that has remained inside you because it was heaped up
out of such blocks that you can no longer
lift them out of yourself without demolishing yourself.
When you've come this far, when everything in you is stone,
wall, staircase, vista, vaulting—then try
to tug away a little with both hands

ein wenig wegzuzerrn mit beiden Händen:
da glänzt es von ganz hohen Gegenständen
und übertrifft dir Atem und Getast.
Hinauf, hinab, Palast steht auf Palast,
Geländer strömen breiter aus Geländern
und tauchen oben auf an solchen Rändern,
daß dich, wie du sie siehst, der Schwindel faßt.
Dabei macht ein Gewölk aus Räucherständern
die Nähe trüb; aber das Fernste zielt
in dich hinein mit seinen graden Strahlen—,
und wenn jetzt Schein aus klaren Flammenschalen
auf langsam nahenden Gewändern spielt:
wie hältst du's aus ?

Sie aber kam und hob
den Blick, um dieses alles anzuschauen.
(Ein Kind, ein kleines Mädchen zwischen Frauen.)
Dann stieg sie ruhig, voller Selbstvertrauen,
dem Aufwand zu, der sich verwöhnt verschob:
So sehr war alles, was die Menschen bauen,
schon überwogen von dem Lob

in ihrem Herzen. Von der Lust
sich hinzugeben an die innern Zeichen:
Die Eltern meinten, sie hinaufzureichen,
der Drohende mit der Juwelenbrust
empfing sie scheinbar: Doch sie ging durch alle,
klein wie sie war, aus jeder Hand hinaus
und in ihr Los, das, höher als die Halle,
schon fertig war, und schwerer als das Haus.

92. Mariae Verkündigung

Nicht daß ein Engel eintrat (das erkenn),
erschreckte sie. Sowenig andre, wenn
ein Sonnenstrahl oder der Mond bei Nacht
in ihrem Zimmer sich zu schaffen macht,
auffahren—, pflegte sie an der Gestalt,
in der ein Engel ging, sich zu entrüsten;
sie ahnte kaum, daß dieser Aufenthalt

the big curtain that's in front of you:
it will shine with very lofty objects,
outdistancing your breath and sense of touch.
Up, down, one palace rests on another,
railings flow more broadly out of railings,
emerging above beside brinks so precipitous
that you get dizzy when you look at them.
At the same time, a cloud rising from censers makes
what is nearby dim; but the farthest distance aims
its straight beams right into you—
and if now a glow from bright bowls of flame
plays over slowly approaching robes:
how will you stand it?

But she came and raised
her eyes to observe all this.
(A child, a little girl amid women.)
Then she ascended calmly, full of self-confidence,
toward that pomp, which moved aside like a spoiled child:
so greatly was everything constructed by man
already outweighed by the praise

in her heart. By the urge
to dedicate herself to the inward signs.
Her parents thought they were handing her up,
the menacing man with jewels on his chest
apparently received her: but she passed through them all,
small as she was, out of every hand
and into her destiny, which, higher than the hall,
was already determined, and heavier than the house.

92. The Annunciation to the Virgin

Not because an angel entered (be aware of this!)
did she get frightened. Just as little as others give a start
when a sunbeam or the moon at night
busies itself in their room,
was she accustomed to be aroused
by the shape assumed by an angel;
she had hardly an inkling that this tarrying

mühsam für Engel ist. (O wenn wir wüßten,
wie rein sie war. Hat eine Hirschkuh nicht,
die, liegend, einmal sie im Wald eräugte,
sich so in sie versehn, daß sich in ihr,
ganz ohne Paarigen, das Einhorn zeugte,
das Tier aus Licht, das reine Tier—.)
Nicht, daß er eintrat, aber daß er dicht,
der Engel, eines Jünglings Angesicht
so zu ihr neigte; daß sein Blick und der,
mit dem sie aufsah, so zusammenschlugen
als wäre draußen plötzlich alles leer
und, was Millionen schauten, trieben, trugen,
hineingedrängt in sie: nur sie und er;
Schaun und Geschautes, Aug und Augenweide
sonst nirgends als an dieser Stelle—; sieh,
dieses erschreckt. Und sie erschraken beide.

Dann sang der Engel seine Melodie.

93. Verkündigung über den Hirten

Seht auf, ihr Männer. Männer dort am Feuer,
die ihr den grenzenlosen Himmel kennt,
Sterndeuter, hierher! Seht, ich bin ein neuer
steigender Stern. Mein ganzes Wesen brennt
und strahlt so stark und ist so ungeheuer
voll Licht, daß mir das tiefe Firmament
nicht mehr genügt. Laßt meinen Glanz hinein
in euer Dasein: Oh, die dunklen Blicke,
die dunklen Herzen, nächtige Geschicke
die euch erfüllen. Hirten, wie allein
bin ich in euch. Auf einmal wird mir Raum.
Stauntet ihr nicht: der große Brotfruchtbaum
warf einen Schatten. Ja, das kam von mir.
Ihr Unerschrockenen, o wüßtet ihr,
wie jetzt auf eurem schauenden Gesichte
die Zukunft scheint. In diesem starken Lichte
wird viel geschehen. Euch vertrau ichs, denn
ihr seid verschwiegen; euch Gradgläubigen
redet hier alles. Glut und Regen spricht,

is troublesome to angels. (Oh, if we only knew
how pure she was! Didn't a doe
that, lying in the woods, once caught sight of her,
become so absorbed in her that, without any mating,
the unicorn was engendered in it,
that animal made of light, the pure animal?)
Not because he entered, but because he came so close,
that angel, bowing a stripling's face
down to her; because his gaze and the one
with which she looked up merged in such a way
that everything outside seemed suddenly empty,
as if all that millions were seeing, doing, bearing
had forced itself into them: there was only she and he;
the view and the viewed, the eye and its delight,
nowhere else than on that spot—see,
that's what's frightening. And they both were frightened.

Then the angel sang his melody.

93. Annunciation to the Shepherds

Look up, men! Men by the fire there,
you who know the boundless sky,
astrologers, look up here! See, I am a new,
rising star. My whole being burns
and beams so strongly and is so enormously
full of light that the high firmament
no longer suffices me. Let me shine into
your existence! Oh, the dark glances,
the dark hearts, the nocturnal destinies
which you are filled with! Shepherds, I am
in you as if all alone. All at once I have space.
Weren't you amazed? The big breadfruit tree
cast a shadow. Yes, it came from me.
Intrepid men, if you only knew
how now on your gazing faces
the future shines! In this strong light
much will happen. I confide it in you, for
you're discreet; to you true believers
everything here speaks. Fire and rain speak,

der Vögel Zug, der Wind und was ihr seid,
keins überwiegt und wächst zur Eitelkeit
sich mästend an. Ihr haltet nicht
die Dinge auf im Zwischenraum der Brust
um sie zu quälen. So wie seine Lust
durch einen Engel strömt, so treibt durch euch
das Irdische. Und wenn ein Dorngesträuch
aufflammte plötzlich, dürfte noch aus ihm
der Ewige euch rufen, Cherubim,
wenn sie geruhten neben eurer Herde
einherzuschreiten, wunderten euch nicht:
ihr stürztet euch auf euer Angesicht,
betetet an und nenntet dies die Erde.

Doch dieses war. Nun soll ein Neues sein,
von dem der Erdkreis ringender sich weitet.
Was ist ein Dörnicht uns: Gott fühlt sich ein
in einer Jungfrau Schooß. Ich bin der Schein
von ihrer Innigkeit, der euch geleitet.

94. Pietà

Jetzt wird mein Elend voll, und namenlos
erfüllt es mich. Ich starre wie des Steins
Inneres starrt.
Hart wie ich bin, weiß ich nur Eins:
Du wurdest groß—
. . . . . . und wurdest groß,
um als zu großer Schmerz
ganz über meines Herzens Fassung
hinauszustehn.
Jetzt liegst du quer durch meinen Schooß,
jetzt kann ich dich nicht mehr
gebären.

95. Die erste [Duineser] Elegie

Wer, wenn ich schriee, hörte mich denn aus der Engel
Ordnungen? und gesetzt selbst, es nähme

the birds' flight, the wind, and all that you are,
none of these preponderates or grows into vanity
by gorging. You don't hold
things back in the interspace of your breast
so you can torment them. Just as an angel's
pleasure flows through him, so does the earthly
surge through you. And if a thornbush
burst suddenly into flame, the Eternal One
could still call out of it to you; if cherubim
condescended to walk
beside your flock, they wouldn't surprise you:
you'd fall to your faces,
worship them, and call this the earth.

But that's in the past. Now there shall be something new
which will make the world widen with a greater struggle.
What's a thornbush to us? God is feeling his way
into a virgin's womb. I am the glow
of her inwardness, conducting you.

94. Pietà

Now my misery becomes full, and inexpressibly
fills me. I am rigid, as the inside
of a stone is rigid.
Hard as I am, I know only one thing:
You grew big—
. . . . . . and grew big
in order to protrude
completely beyond my heart's frame,
as a grief too great.
Now you lie across my lap,
now I can no longer give you
birth.

95. The First [Duino] Elegy

Who, then, were I to cry out, would hear me, who among the angels'
ranks? And even assuming that one would

einer mich plötzlich ans Herz: ich verginge von seinem
stärkeren Dasein. Denn das Schöne ist nichts
als des Schrecklichen Anfang, den wir noch grade ertragen,
und wir bewundern es so, weil es gelassen verschmäht,
uns zu zerstören. Ein jeder Engel ist schrecklich.
    Und so verhalt ich mich denn und verschlucke den Lockruf
dunkelen Schluchzens. Ach, wen vermögen
wir denn zu brauchen? Engel nicht, Menschen nicht,
und die findigen Tiere merken es schon,
daß wir nicht sehr verläßlich zu Haus sind
in der gedeuteten Welt. Es bleibt uns vielleicht
irgend ein Baum an dem Abhang, daß wir ihn täglich
wiedersähen; es bleibt uns die Straße von gestern
und das verzogene Treusein einer Gewohnheit,
der es bei uns gefiel, und so blieb sie und ging nicht.
    O und die Nacht, die Nacht, wenn der Wind voller Weltraum
uns am Angesicht zehrt—, wem bliebe sie nicht, die ersehnte,
sanft enttäuschende, welche dem einzelnen Herzen
mühsam bevorsteht. Ist sie den Liebenden leichter?
Ach, sie verdecken sich nur mit einander ihr Los.
    Weißt du's *noch* nicht? Wirf aus den Armen die Leere
zu den Räumen hinzu, die wir atmen; vielleicht daß die Vögel
die erweiterte Luft fühlen mit innigerm Flug.

    Ja, die Frühlinge brauchten dich wohl. Es muteten manche
Sterne dir zu, daß du sie spürtest. Es hob
sich eine Woge heran im Vergangenen, oder
da du vorüberkamst am geöffneten Fenster,
gab eine Geige sich hin. Das alles war Auftrag.
Aber bewältigtest du's? Warst du nicht immer
noch von Erwartung zerstreut, als kündigte alles
eine Geliebte dir an? (Wo willst du sie bergen,
da doch die großen fremden Gedanken bei dir
aus und ein gehn und öfters bleiben bei Nacht.)
Sehnt es dich aber, so singe die Liebenden; lange
noch nicht unsterblich genug ist ihr berühmtes Gefühl.
Jene, du neidest sie fast, Verlassenen, die du
so viel liebender fandst als die Gestillten. Beginn
immer von neuem die nie zu erreichende Preisung;
denk: es erhält sich der Held, selbst der Untergang war ihm
nur ein Vorwand, zu sein: seine letzte Geburt.

suddenly take me to his heart: I'd perish from his
stronger existence. For the beautiful is nothing other
than the beginning of the frightful, which we can just still abide,
and we admire it as we do because it calmly scorns
to destroy us. Each and every angel is frightful.
   And so I restrain myself and repress the luring call
of dark sobbing. Ah, whom, then, are we able
to use? Not angels, not people,
and the clever animals are already observing
that we aren't very reliably at home
in the world that we interpret. Perhaps we still have
some tree on the slope to look at again
every day; we still have yesterday's street
and the pampered loyalty of a habit
that enjoyed being with us and thus remained and didn't depart.
   Oh, and the night, the night, when the space-filled wind
nibbles at our face—who lacks the night, so longed for,
gently disabusing, which is industriously ready for
the lonely heart? Is it easier to bear for lovers?
Ah, they merely use each other to hide their fate from themselves.
   Don't you know it *yet*? Fling that emptiness from your arms
into the space that we breathe; perhaps the birds
will feel the expanded air in a more inward flight.

   Yes, the springtimes did need you. Many stars expected
you to notice them. A wave
rose up within the past, or else,
when you passed by the open window,
a violin surrendered itself. All that was an assignment.
But did you accomplish it? Weren't you always
still distracted by expectancy, as if everything announced
a beloved to you? (Where will you keep her safe,
seeing that those great, strange thoughts in you
go in and out and often remain at night?)
But if you have the urge, sing about lovers; their
famous emotion is not yet immortal enough by far.
You almost envy those who were forsaken, whom you
found so much more loving than the satisfied ones. Begin
over and over again the praise that can never be finished;
recall that the hero endures; even his destruction was
only a pretext for him to live on: his final birth.

Aber die Liebenden nimmt die erschöpfte Natur
in sich zurück, als wären nicht zweimal die Kräfte,
dieses zu leisten. Hast du der Gaspara Stampa
denn genügend gedacht, daß irgend ein Mädchen,
dem der Geliebte entging, am gesteigerten Beispiel
dieser Liebenden fühlt: daß ich würde wie sie?
Sollen nicht endlich uns diese ältesten Schmerzen
fruchtbarer werden ? Ist es nicht Zeit, daß wir liebend
uns vom Geliebten befrein und es bebend bestehn:
wie der Pfeil die Sehne besteht, um gesammelt im Absprung
mehr zu sein als er selbst. Denn Bleiben ist nirgends.

Stimmen, Stimmen. Höre, mein Herz, wie sonst nur
Heilige hörten: daß sie der riesige Ruf
aufhob vom Boden; sie aber knieten,
Unmögliche, weiter und achtetens nicht:
So waren sie hörend. Nicht, daß du *Gottes* ertrügest
die Stimme, bei weitem. Aber das Wehende höre,
die ununterbrochene Nachricht, die aus Stille sich bildet.
Es rauscht jetzt von jenen jungen Toten zu dir.
Wo immer du eintratst, redete nicht in Kirchen
zu Rom und Neapel ruhig ihr Schicksal dich an?
Oder es trug eine Inschrift sich erhaben dir auf,
wie neulich die Tafel in Santa Maria Formosa.
Was sie mir wollen? leise soll ich des Unrechts
Anschein abtun, der ihrer Geister
reine Bewegung manchmal ein wenig behindert.

Freilich ist es seltsam, die Erde nicht mehr zu bewohnen,
kaum erlernte Gebräuche nicht mehr zu üben,
Rosen, und andern eigens versprechenden Dingen
nicht die Bedeutung menschlicher Zukunft zu geben;
das, was man war in unendlich ängstlichen Händen,
nicht mehr zu sein, und selbst den eigenen Namen
wegzulassen wie ein zerbrochenes Spielzeug.
Seltsam, die Wünsche nicht weiterzuwünschen. Seltsam,
alles, was sich bezog, so lose im Raume
flattern zu sehen. Und das Totsein ist mühsam
und voller Nachholn, daß man allmählich ein wenig
Ewigkeit spürt.—Aber Lebendige machen
alle den Fehler, daß sie zu stark unterscheiden.

But exhausted Nature resorbs lovers into herself
as if the strength to accomplish it
couldn't be mustered up twice. Have you thought enough
about Gaspara Stampa so that some girl
who has lost her lover, by the heightened example
of that loving woman, may feel she'd want to become like her?
Shall these ancient sorrows not finally become
more profitable to us? Isn't it time for us lovingly
to free ourselves of our loved one and endure it tremblingly?—
as the arrow endures the string, so that, with a concentrated takeoff,
it can be *more* than itself. For there is nowhere to tarry.

Voices, voices. Listen, my heart, the way only
saints used to listen: the titanic summons
lifted them from the ground; but they, the impossible ones,
kept on kneeling and paid no heed to it:
that was how *they* listened. Not that you'd endure *God's*
voice, not by a long shot. But hear this wafting,
this uninterrupted message which is shaped from silence.
It now resounds, coming to you from those youthful dead.
Wherever you entered, didn't their fate speak to you
quietly in churches in Rome and Naples?
Or else an inscription impressed itself grandly on you as a task,
like that plaque recently in Santa Maria Formosa.
What do they want of me? That I should gently throw off
the semblance of injustice that sometimes slightly impedes
the pure motion of their spirits.

Of course, it's odd no longer to inhabit the earth,
no longer to practice customs you've just barely learned,
not to give to roses and other specially promising things
the significance of human future;
no longer to be that which you were in infinitely
anxious hands, and even to relinquish
your own name like a broken toy.
Odd not to keep on wishing your wishes. Odd
to see all those once interconnected things fluttering
so loosely in space. And being dead is laborious
and full of catching up, so you can gradually feel
a little bit of eternity. —But all living people
commit the error of making too sharp distinctions.

Engel (sagt man) wüßten oft nicht, ob sie unter
Lebenden gehn oder Toten. Die ewige Strömung
reißt durch beide Bereiche alle Alter
immer mit sich und übertönt sie in beiden.

Schließlich brauchen sie uns nicht mehr, die Früheentrückten,
man entwöhnt sich des Irdischen sanft, wie man den Brüsten
milde der Mutter entwächst. Aber wir, die so große
Geheimnisse brauchen, denen aus Trauer so oft
seliger Fortschritt entspringt—: *könnten* wir sein ohne sie?
Ist die Sage umsonst, daß einst in der Klage um Linos
wagende erste Musik dürre Erstarrung durchdrang;
daß erst im erschrockenen Raum, dem ein beinah göttlicher Jüngling
plötzlich für immer enttrat, das Leere in jene
Schwingung geriet, die uns jetzt hinreißt und tröstet und hilft.

96. Die zweite Elegie

Jeder Engel ist schrecklich. Und dennoch, weh mir,
ansing ich euch, fast tödliche Vögel der Seele,
wissend um euch. Wohin sind die Tage Tobiae,
da der Strahlendsten einer stand an der einfachen Haustür,
zur Reise ein wenig verkleidet und schon nicht mehr furchtbar;
(Jüngling dem Jüngling, wie er neugierig hinaussah).
Träte der Erzengel jetzt, der gefährliche, hinter den Sternen
eines Schrittes nur nieder und herwärts: hochauf-
schlagend erschlüg uns das eigene Herz. Wer seid ihr?

Frühe Geglückte, ihr Verwöhnten der Schöpfung,
Höhenzüge, morgenrötliche Grate
aller Erschaffung,—Pollen der blühenden Gottheit,
Gelenke des Lichtes, Gänge, Treppen, Throne,
Räume aus Wesen, Schilde aus Wonne, Tumulte
stürmisch entzückten Gefühls und plötzlich, einzeln,
Spiegel: die die entströmte eigene Schönheit
wiederschöpfen zurück in das eigene Antlitz.

Denn wir, wo wir fühlen, verflüchtigen; ach wir
atmen uns aus und dahin; von Holzglut zu Holzglut
geben wir schwächern Geruch. Da sagt uns wohl einer:
ja, du gehst mir ins Blut, dieses Zimmer, der Frühling

It's said that angels often don't know whether
they're among the living or the dead. The eternal current
keeps on tearing those of all ages along with it
through both realms, drowning out their voices in both.

Finally, those who were taken away young don't need us any more,
they grow gently disaccustomed to earthly things, just as we
calmly grow too big to need our mother's breasts. But we who need
such great mysteries, from which through sorrow so often
blissful progress arises—*could* we exist without them?
Is that legend vain which tells how once, in laments for Linos,
the first music boldly penetrated withered petrifaction? —
how it was only in that frightened space, which an almost divine youth
suddenly left forever, that emptiness entered into that
vibration which now enraptures, comforts, and helps us?

96. The Second Elegy

Every angel is terrifying. And yet, woe is me,
I address you in song, you almost deadly birds of the soul,
knowing what you are. Where have the days of Tobias gone,
when one of the most radiant stood at the simple house door,
somewhat disguised as a traveler and already no longer frightful
(as a youth to the youth who looked out in curiosity)?
Were the dangerous archangel now, behind the stars,
to take only one step down and toward us, our own heart
would start to beat tremendously and slay us. Who are you, angels?

Early successes of God, pampered ones of Creation,
mountain ranges, ridges ruddy with morning
among created beings—pollen of the blossoming Godhead,
articulations of light, corridors, stairways, thrones,
spaces formed from essence, shields formed from bliss, uproars
of stormily enraptured emotion, and suddenly, individually,
mirrors: which resorb their own irradiated
beauty into their own countenance.

For we are volatilized when we feel deeply; alas, we
breathe ourselves out and away; from one wood-ember to another
we give off a weaker smell. Someone may say to us:
"Yes, you get into my blood, this room, the springtime

füllt sich mit dir . . . Was hilfts, er kann uns nicht halten,
wir schwinden in ihm und um ihn. Und jene, die schön sind,
o wer hält sie zurück? Unaufhörlich steht Anschein
auf in ihrem Gesicht und geht fort. Wie Tau von dem Frühgras
hebt sich das Unsre von uns, wie die Hitze von einem
heißen Gericht. O Lächeln, wohin? O Aufschaun:
neue, warme, entgehende Welle des Herzens—;
weh mir: wir *sinds* doch. Schmeckt denn der Weltraum,
in den wir uns lösen, nach uns? Fangen die Engel
wirklich nur Ihriges auf, ihnen Entströmtes,
oder ist manchmal, wie aus Versehen, ein wenig
unseres Wesens dabei? Sind wir in ihre
Züge soviel nur gemischt wie das Vage in die Gesichter
schwangerer Frauen? Sie merken es nicht in dem Wirbel
ihrer Rückkehr zu sich. (Wie sollten sie's merken.)

Liebende könnten, verstünden sie's, in der Nachtluft
wunderlich reden. Denn es scheint, daß uns alles
verheimlicht. Siehe, die Bäume *sind;* die Häuser,
die wir bewohnen, bestehn noch. Wir nur
ziehen allem vorbei wie ein luftiger Austausch.
Und alles ist einig, uns zu verschweigen, halb als
Schande vielleicht und halb als unsägliche Hoffnung.

Liebende, euch, ihr in einander Genügten,
frag ich nach uns. Ihr greift euch. Habt ihr Beweise?
Seht, mir geschiehts, daß meine Hände einander
inne werden oder daß mein gebrauchtes
Gesicht in ihnen sich schont. Das giebt mir ein wenig
Empfindung. Doch wer wagte darum schon zu *sein?*
Ihr aber, die ihr im Entzücken des anderen
zunehmt, bis er euch überwältigt
anfleht: nicht *mehr*—; die ihr unter den Händen
euch reichlicher werdet wie Traubenjahre;
die ihr manchmal vergeht, nur weil der andre
ganz überhand nimmt: euch frag ich nach uns. Ich weiß,
ihr berührt euch so selig, weil die Liebkosung verhält,
weil die Stelle nicht schwindet, die ihr, Zärtliche,
zudeckt; weil ihr darunter das reine
Dauern verspürt. So versprecht ihr euch Ewigkeit fast
von der Umarmung. Und doch, wenn ihr der ersten
Blicke Schrecken besteht und die Sehnsucht am Fenster,

becomes full of you."...What's the good? It can't retain us,
we evaporate in it and around it. And those who are beautiful,
oh, who can hold onto *them*? Endlessly semblance
arises in their faces and departs. Like dew from morning grass,
what belongs to us abandons us like the steam from a
hot dish of food. O smiles, where do you go? O upward glances:
you fresh, warm, elusive wave in the heart—
woe is me, we *are* that after all. Does the world space, then,
into which we dissolve taste of us? Do the angels really
intercept only what's theirs, what has radiated from them,
or is there sometimes, as if by mistake, a little
of our essence present? Are we mingled in their
features only to the extent that vagueness is mingled in the faces
of pregnant women? They don't notice it in the whirlwind
of their return to themselves. (How could they notice it?)

Lovers, if they knew how, could say wondrous things
in the night air. For it seems that everything keeps us
a secret. See: trees *exist*; the houses
we live in still stand. Only we
pass by everything like an airy exchange.
And everything conspires to keep silent about us, partly
from shame perhaps, partly from inexpressible hope.

   Lovers, you that have found contentment in each other,
I ask you about us. You grasp each other. Do you have proof?
Look: it happens at times that my hands become
aware of each other or that my used-up
face is handled gently by them. That affords me some
sensation. But who, just because of that, would dare to *exist*?
Yet you, you that grow bigger in the rapture
of your partner until, overcome, he or she
implores you: "No more!" You that in each other's hands
become more ample to each other like good grape harvests;
you that sometimes swoon merely because your partner
becomes altogether prevalent: I ask you about us. I know
you touch each other so blissfully because caresses are sustained,
because that spot doesn't evaporate which you tenderly
cover; because beneath all this you detect
pure permanency. So you all but promise each other eternity
from your embraces. And yet, once you've undergone
the terror of the first glances and the longing by the window

und den ersten gemeinsamen Gang, *ein* Mal durch den Garten:
Liebende, *seid* ihrs dann noch? Wenn ihr einer dem andern
euch an den Mund hebt und ansetzt—: Getränk an Getränk:
o wie entgeht dann der Trinkende seltsam der Handlung.

Erstaunte euch nicht auf attischen Stelen die Vorsicht
menschlicher Geste? war nicht Liebe und Abschied
so leicht auf die Schultern gelegt, als wär es aus anderm
Stoffe gemacht als bei uns? Gedenkt euch der Hände,
wie sie drucklos beruhen, obwohl in den Torsen die Kraft steht.
Diese Beherrschten wußten damit: so weit sind wirs,
dieses ist unser, uns *so* zu berühren; stärker
stemmen die Götter uns an. Doch dies ist Sache der Götter.

Fänden auch wir ein reines, verhaltenes, schmales
Menschliches, einen unseren Streifen Fruchtlands
zwischen Strom und Gestein. Denn das eigene Herz übersteigt uns
noch immer wie jene. Und wir können ihm nicht mehr
nachschaun in Bilder, die es besänftigen, noch in
göttliche Körper, in denen es größer sich mäßigt.

97. Die Neunte Elegie

Warum, wenn es angeht, also die Frist des Daseins
hinzubringen, als Lorbeer, ein wenig dunkler als alles
andere Grün, mit kleinen Wellen an jedem
Blattrand (wie eines Windes Lächeln)—: warum dann
Menschliches müssen—und, Schicksal vermeidend,
sich sehnen nach Schicksal? . . .

                Oh, *nicht*, weil Glück *ist*,
dieser voreilige Vorteil eines nahen Verlusts.
Nicht aus Neugier, oder zur Übung des Herzens,
das auch im Lorbeer *wäre* . . . . .

Aber weil Hiersein viel ist, und weil uns scheinbar
alles das Hiesige braucht, dieses Schwindende, das
seltsam uns angeht. Uns, die Schwindendsten. *Ein* Mal
jedes, nur *ein* Mal. *Ein* Mal und nichtmehr. Und wir auch
ein Mal. Nie wieder. Aber dieses
ein Mal gewesen zu sein, wenn auch nur *ein* Mal:
irdisch gewesen zu sein, scheint nicht widerrufbar.

and the first walk together, *once* through the garden:
lovers, *are* you then still the same? When you raise each other
to your mouth and set each other to your lips—drink to drink—
oh, how oddly then the one who drinks escapes the act!

Haven't you been surprised to see, on Attic steles, how
cautious people's gestures are? Weren't love and leavetaking
laid so lightly on their shoulders as if made of
other material than they are with us? Recall how the hands
repose without pressure, though there's strength in the torsos.
Those self-controlled people therefore knew: "We've come this far,
this behooves us, to touch each other *thus;* the gods
lean against us harder. But that's the gods' affair."

If only we, too, could find a pure, reserved, narrow
human attitude, a strip of fertile land that would be ours
between river and rocks! For our own heart still
exceeds us, as theirs did. And we can no longer
gaze after it, at pictures that calm it, or into
godlike bodies in which it becomes more nobly moderate.

97. The Ninth Elegy

Why, when it concerns us to live out the term
of our existence just like laurel, a little darker than any
other green, with little waves on every
leaf's edge (like a wind's smile) —why then
are we forced to be human—and, avoiding fate,
to long for fate? . . .

        Oh, *not* because happiness *exists*,
that too-hasty profit before some approaching loss.
Not out of curiosity, or as training for the heart
which *would be so* even in the laurel. . . ,

but because to be here takes a lot, and because apparently
everything here needs us, this evaporating world that
oddly concerns us. Us, the most fleeting thing of all. *Once*
each thing exists, just once. Once and no more. And we, too,
just once. Never again. But this
having-been once, even if only once—
having been *of the earth*—seems irrevocable.

Und so drängen wir uns und wollen es leisten,
wollens enthalten in unsern einfachen Händen,
im überfüllteren Blick und im sprachlosen Herzen.
Wollen es werden.—Wem es geben? Am liebsten
alles behalten für immer . . . Ach, in den andern Bezug,
wehe, was nimmt man hinüber? Nicht das Anschaun, das hier
langsam erlernte, und kein hier Ereignetes. Keins.
Also die Schmerzen. Also vor allem das Schwersein,
also der Liebe lange Erfahrung,—also
lauter Unsägliches. Aber später,
unter den Sternen, was solls: *die* sind *besser* unsäglich.
Bringt doch der Wanderer auch vom Hange des Bergrands
nicht eine Hand voll Erde ins Tal, die Allen unsägliche, sondern
ein erworbenes Wort, reines, den gelben und blaun
Enzian. Sind wir vielleicht *hier*, um zu sagen: Haus,
Brücke, Brunnen, Tor, Krug, Obstbaum, Fenster,—
höchstens: Säule, Turm . . . . aber zu *sagen*, verstehs,
oh zu sagen *so*, wie selber die Dinge niemals
innig meinten zu sein. Ist nicht die heimliche List
dieser verschwiegenen Erde, wenn sie die Liebenden drängt,
daß sich in ihrem Gefühl jedes und jedes entzückt?
Schwelle: was ists für zwei
Liebende, daß sie die eigne ältere Schwelle der Tür
ein wenig verbrauchen, auch sie, nach den vielen vorher
und vor den Künftigen . . . . , leicht.

Hier ist des *Säglichen* Zeit, *hier* seine Heimat.
Sprich und bekenn. Mehr als je
fallen die Dinge dahin, die erlebbaren, denn,
was sie verdrängend ersetzt, ist ein Tun ohne Bild.
Tun unter Krusten, die willig zerspringen, sobald
innen das Handeln entwächst und sich anders begrenzt.
Zwischen den Hämmern besteht
unser Herz, wie die Zunge
zwischen den Zähnen, die doch,
dennoch, die preisende bleibt.

Preise dem Engel die Welt, nicht die unsägliche, *ihm*
kannst du nicht großtun mit herrlich Erfühltem; im Weltall,
wo er fühlender fühlt, bist du ein Neuling. Drum zeig
ihm das Einfache, das, von Geschlecht zu Geschlechtern gestaltet,
als ein Unsriges lebt, neben der Hand und im Blick.

And so we push ourselves on, desiring to accomplish it,
we want to contain it in our simple hands,
in a more abundant gaze and in our speechless heart.
We want to become it. —To whom are we to give it? Best of all,
to keep everything forever . . . Ah, into that other condition,
alas, what do we take with us? Not our way of seeing things,
which we slowly learned here, not one thing that occurred here. Not one.
Our sorrows, then. Then, especially our heaviness;
then, our long experience of love—then,
only inexpressible things. But later,
among the stars, what good is it? *They* are *better* left unexpressed.
After all, a traveler, too, brings from the slope of the foothills
back to the valley not a handful of earth, inexpressible to all,
but a word he has acquired, a pure one, the yellow and blue
gentian. Are we perhaps *here* so we can say, "House,
bridge, well, gate, jug, fruit tree, window,"
or at best, "column, tower" . . . but to *say* (understand me),
oh, to say them on such a way as the things themselves never
inwardly intended to be? Isn't it the secret ruse
of this taciturn earth, when it urges lovers on,
to have each and every one take delight in himself through his feelings?
Threshold: what is it to two
lovers if they wear out somewhat their own older
threshold, they, too, after the many who preceded
and before those to come . . . lightly?

Here is the time of the *expressible*, its home is *here*.
Speak and confess. More than ever
the things that can be experienced are falling away, for
what supplants and replaces them is an imageless activity.
An activity overlain with crusts which gladly crack as soon as
the actions within outgrow it and redefine their limits.
Between the hammers
our heart endures, like the tongue
between our teeth, which
nevertheless continues to praise.

Praise the world to the angel, not the inexpressible world, to *him*
you can't show off with wonderful things you've felt; in the universe
in which *he* feels more feelingly you're a newcomer. So show
him simple things, which, formed from generation to generation,
live as something of us, near to hand and in our sight.

Sag ihm die Dinge. Er wird staunender stehn; wie du standest
bei dem Seiler in Rom, oder beim Töpfer am Nil.
Zeig ihm, wie glücklich ein Ding sein kann, wie schuldlos und unser,
wie selbst das klagende Leid rein zur Gestalt sich entschließt,
dient als ein Ding, oder stirbt in ein Ding—, und jenseits
selig der Geige entgeht.—Und diese, von Hingang
lebenden Dinge verstehn, daß du sie rühmst; vergänglich,
traun sie ein Rettendes uns, den Vergänglichsten, zu.
Wollen, wir sollen sie ganz im unsichtbarn Herzen verwandeln
in—o unendlich—in uns! Wer wir am Ende auch seien.

Erde, ist es nicht dies, was du willst: *unsichtbar*
in uns erstehn?—Ist es dein Traum nicht,
einmal unsichtbar zu sein?—Erde! unsichtbar!
Was, wenn Verwandlung nicht, ist dein drängender Auftrag?
Erde, du liebe, ich will. Oh glaub, es bedürfte
nicht deiner Frühlinge mehr, mich dir zu gewinnen—, *einer*,
ach, ein einziger ist schon dem Blute zu viel.
Namenlos bin ich zu dir entschlossen, von weit her.
Immer warst du im Recht, und dein heiliger Einfall
ist der vertrauliche Tod.

Siehe, ich lebe. Woraus? Weder Kindheit noch Zukunft
werden weniger . . . . . Überzähliges Dasein
entspringt mir im Herzen.

98. Die zehnte Elegie

Daß ich dereinst, an dem Ausgang der grimmigen Einsicht,
Jubel und Ruhm aufsinge zustimmenden Engeln.
Daß von den klar geschlagenen Hämmern des Herzens
keiner versage an weichen, zweifelnden oder
reißenden Saiten. Daß mich mein strömendes Antlitz
glänzender mache; daß das unscheinbare Weinen
blühe. O wie werdet ihr dann, Nächte, mir lieb sein,
gehärmte. Daß ich euch knieender nicht, untröstliche Schwestern,
hinnahm, nicht in euer gelöstes
Haar mich gelöster ergab. Wir, Vergeuder der Schmerzen.
Wie wir sie absehn voraus, in die traurige Dauer,
ob sie nicht enden vielleicht. Sie aber sind ja

Tell him of the things. He'll stand there more amazed, as you stood
next to the ropemaker in Rome or the potter by the Nile.
Show him how happy a thing can be, how guiltless and how much ours,
how even a sorrowful pain is resolved to assume a pure shape,
serves as a thing, or dies into a thing—and, in the beyond,
blissfully escapes the violin. —And these things, which live
by perishing, understand your praising them; mortal,
they believe us, the most mortal, capable of rescuing them somehow.
They want us to transform them completely in our invisible heart
into—oh, eternally! —into ourselves! Whoever we might actually be.

Earth, isn't that what you want: to be resurrected
invisibly in us? —Isn't it your dream
to be invisible at last? Earth! invisible!
What is your urgent errand if it's not transformation?
Earth, you dear one, I'm willing. Oh, believe me, there's no need
any longer for your springtimes to win me over to you—*one*,
ah, just one is already too rich for my blood.
I am unutterably resolved to be yours, and I have long been.
You were always right, and the holy idea that came to you
is friendly death.

See, I live. On what? Neither childhood nor future
grows less . . . . A surplus of existence
wells up in my heart.

98. The Tenth Elegy

May I some day, on exiting from angry insight,
sing joy and praise to acquiescent angels!
May none of the clearly tapped hammers of my heart
fail me because the piano strings are weak and hesitant,
or tear! May my streaming face
make me shine more! May inconspicuous weeping
blossom! O nights, how dear to me you'll become then,
aggrieved ones! Because, inconsolable sisters, I didn't accept
you more often on my knees, didn't surrender myself more detachedly
to your unbound hair. We squanderers of sorrows!
How we foresee them, looking past them into mournful duration,
wondering whether they'll ever end! But in fact they're

unser winterwähriges Laub, unser dunkeles Sinngrün,
eine der Zeiten des heimlichen Jahres—, nicht nur
Zeit—, sind Stelle, Siedelung, Lager, Boden, Wohnort.

Freilich, wehe, wie fremd sind die Gassen der Leid-Stadt,
wo in der falschen, aus Übertönung gemachten
Stille, stark, aus der Gußform des Leeren der Ausguß
prahlt: der vergoldete Lärm, das platzende Denkmal.
O, wie spurlos zerträte ein Engel ihnen den Trostmarkt,
den die Kirche begrenzt, ihre fertig gekaufte:
reinlich und zu und enttäuscht wie ein Postamt am Sonntag.
Draußen aber kräuseln sich immer die Ränder von Jahrmarkt.
Schaukeln der Freiheit! Taucher und Gaukler des Eifers!
Und des behübschten Glücks figürliche Schießstatt,
wo es zappelt von Ziel und sich blechern benimmt,
wenn ein Geschickterer trifft. Von Beifall zu Zufall
taumelt er weiter; denn Buden jeglicher Neugier
werben, trommeln und plärrn. Für Erwachsene aber
ist noch besonders zu sehn, wie das Geld sich vermehrt, anatomisch,
nicht zur Belustigung nur: der Geschlechtsteil des Gelds,
alles, das Ganze, der Vorgang—, das unterrichtet und macht
fruchtbar . . . .
. . . . Oh aber gleich darüber hinaus,
hinter der letzten Planke, beklebt mit Plakaten des >Todlos<,
jenes bitteren Biers, das den Trinkenden süß scheint,
wenn sie immer dazu frische Zerstreuungen kaun . . . ,
gleich im Rücken der Planke, gleich dahinter, ists *wirklich.*
Kinder spielen, und Liebende halten einander,—abseits,
ernst, im ärmlichen Gras, und Hunde haben Natur.
Weiter noch zieht es den Jüngling; vielleicht, daß er eine junge
Klage liebt. . . . . . Hinter ihr her kommt er in Wiesen. Sie sagt:
—Weit. Wir wohnen dort draußen . . . . Wo? Und der Jüngling
folgt. Ihn rührt ihre Haltung. Die Schulter, der Hals—, vielleicht
ist sie von herrlicher Herkunft. Aber er läßt sie, kehrt um,
wendet sich, winkt . . . Was solls? Sie ist eine Klage.

Nur die jungen Toten, im ersten Zustand
zeitlosen Gleichmuts, dem der Entwöhnung,
folgen ihr liebend. Mädchen

our winter-lasting foliage, our dark periwinkle,[8]
one of the seasons of the secret year—not only
time—they're place, settlement, camp, homeground, domicile.

To be sure, alas! how strange are the streets of Sorrowtown,
where in the false silence due to the drowning out
of other sounds, the casting from the mold of emptiness mightily
boasts: the gilded noise, the exploding monument.
Oh, how an angel would crush without a trace their solace-market,
which borders on their ready-bought church,
tidy and shut and disappointed as a post office on Sunday!
But, outside, the edges of the fairground are always rippling.
Seesaws of freedom! Divers and jugglers of enthusiasm!
And the figure-filled shooting gallery of prettified happiness,
where it wriggles from the target and acts like a tin sheet
when a more skillful man hits the mark! From applause to chance
he reels onward; for booths appealing to every curiosity
spiel, drum and bawl. But for adults there's yet
the special attraction of money multiplying, anatomically,
not merely as a pastime: the genitals of money,
everything, the whole thing, the process—it's instructive and makes
you fertile . . . .
. . . Oh, but right past that,
behind the last billboard, pasted up with posters for "Deathless,"
that bitter beer which tastes sweet to the drinker
if he always chews on fresh distractions along with it. . . ,
right in back of the board, right behind it, is *reality*.
Children play and lovers hold each other—off to the side,
earnestly, in the scanty grass, and dogs answer Nature's call.
The youth is allured even farther; perhaps he loves a young
lament. . . . He follows her into meadows. She says:
"It's far. We live way out there." "Where?" And the youth
follows. He's struck by her bearing. Her shoulders, her neck—perhaps
she's of noble ancestry. But he leaves her, turns around,
looks back, waves. . . . What's the good? She's a lament.

Only the youthful dead, in the earliest state
of timeless equanimity, that of growing disaccustomed,
follow her amorously. Girls

---

[8]A word play on "the dark greenness of our meaning."

wartet sie ab und befreundet sie. Zeigt ihnen leise,
was sie an sich hat. Perlen des Leids und die feinen
Schleier der Duldung.—Mit Jünglingen geht sie
schweigend.

Aber dort, wo sie wohnen, im Tal, der Älteren eine, der Klagen,
nimmt sich des Jünglinges an, wenn er fragt:—Wir waren,
sagt sie, ein Großes Geschlecht, einmal, wir Klagen. Die Väter
trieben den Bergbau dort in dem großen Gebirg; bei Menschen
findest du manchmal ein Stück geschliffenes Ur-Leid
oder, aus altem Vulkan, schlackig versteinerten Zorn.
Ja, das stammte von dort. Einst waren wir reich.—

Und sie leitet ihn leicht durch die weite Landschaft der Klagen,
zeigt ihm die Säulen der Tempel oder die Trümmer
jener Burgen, von wo Klage-Fürsten das Land
einstens weise beherrscht. Zeigt ihm die hohen
Tränenbäume und Felder blühender Wehmut,
(Lebendige kennen sie nur als sanftes Blattwerk);
zeigt ihm die Tiere der Trauer, weidend,—und manchmal
schreckt ein Vogel und zieht, flach ihnen fliegend durchs Aufschaun,
weithin das schriftliche Bild seines vereinsamten Schreis.—
Abends führt sie ihn hin zu den Gräbern der Alten
aus dem Klage-Geschlecht, den Sibyllen und Warn-Herrn.
Naht aber Nacht, so wandeln sie leiser, und bald
mondets empor, das über Alles
wachende Grab-Mal. Brüderlich jenem am Nil,
der erhabene Sphinx—: der verschwiegenen Kammer
Antlitz.
Und sie staunen dem krönlichen Haupt, das für immer,
schweigend, der Menschen Gesicht
auf die Waage der Sterne gelegt.

Nicht erfaßt es sein Blick, im Frühtod
schwindelnd. Aber ihr Schaun,
hinter dem Pschent-Rand hervor, scheucht es die Eule. Und sie,
streifend im langsamen Abstrich die Wange entlang,
jene der reifesten Rundung,
zeichnet weich in das neue
Totengehör, über ein doppelt
aufgeschlagenes Blatt, den unbeschreiblichen Umriß.

Und höher, die Sterne. Neue. Die Sterne des Leidlands.
Langsam nennt sie die Klage:—Hier,

she waits for and befriends. Gently shows them
what she's wearing. Pearls of sorrow and the thin
veils of forbearance.—With young men she walks
in silence.

But there where they dwell, in the valley, one of the elder laments
replies to the youth when he asks questions. "We were,"
she says, "a powerful family once, we laments. Our ancestors
worked mines there in the big mountain range; in people's homes
you sometimes find a piece of polished primeval sorrow
or, from an old volcano, wrath petrified into slag.
Yes, that came from there. We were once rich."

And she lightly leads him through the wide landscape of the laments,
shows him the columns of the temples or the ruins
of those fortresses from which lament-princes once wisely
controlled the land. Shows him the tall
tear-trees and fields of blossoming wistfulness
(the living know it only as gentle foliage);
shows him the animals of grief, grazing—and at times
a bird wakes up and, flying low across their upward gazes,
draws in the distance the written image of its isolated cry. —
In the evening she leads him to the tombs of the ancients
of the lament family, the sibyls and prophets of doom.
But, as night nears, they walk more quietly, and soon
it rises like a moon, that monument which watches
over it all. A brother to the one by the Nile,
the sublime Sphinx: the face of the concealed
chambers.
And they marvel at the crowned head which, for all time,
in silence, has placed the human face
in the balance with the stars.

His eyes, dizzy in his premature death, can't
take it in. But their gazing
shoos out an owl from behind the edge of the pschent. And,
brushing against the statue's cheek in its slow swoop,
the most roundly ripened cheek, it
softly inscribes into the fresh
dead-man's hearing, across a pair of
opened pages, that indescribable contour.

And, above, the stars. New ones. The stars of Sorrowland.
The lament names them slowly: "Here,

siehe: den *Reiter,* den *Stab,* und das vollere Sternbild
nennen sie: *Fruchtkranz.* Dann, weiter, dem Pol zu:
Wiege; Weg; Das Brennende Buch; Puppe; Fenster.
Aber im südlichen Himmel, rein wie im Innern
einer gesegneten Hand, das klar erglänzende >*M*<,
das die Mütter bedeutet . . . .—

Doch der Tote muß fort, und schweigend bringt ihn die ältere
Klage bis an die Talschlucht,
wo es schimmert im Mondschein:
die Quelle der Freude. In Ehrfurcht
nennt sie sie, sagt:—Bei den Menschen
ist sie ein tragender Strom.—

Stehn am Fuß des Gebirgs.
Und da umarmt sie ihn, weinend.

Einsam steigt er dahin, in die Berge des Ur-Leids.
Und nicht einmal sein Schritt klingt aus dem tonlosen Los.

                              ०

Aber erweckten sie uns, die unendlich Toten, ein Gleichnis,
siehe, sie zeigten vielleicht auf die Kätzchen der leeren
Hasel, die hängenden, oder
meinten den Regen, der fällt auf dunkles Erdreich im Frühjahr.—

Und wir, die an *steigendes* Glück
denken, empfänden die Rührung,
die uns beinah bestürzt,
wenn ein Glückliches *fällt.*

99. "Da stieg ein Baum. O reine Übersteigung!"

Da stieg ein Baum. O reine Übersteigung!
O Orpheus singt! O hoher Baum im Ohr!
Und alles schwieg. Doch selbst in der Verschweigung
ging neuer Anfang, Wink und Wandlung vor.

Tiere aus Stille drangen aus dem klaren
gelösten Wald von Lager und Genist;
und da ergab sich, daß sie nicht aus List
und nicht aus Angst in sich so leise waren,

sondern aus Hören. Brüllen, Schrei, Geröhr
schien klein in ihren Herzen. Und wo eben

look: the Horseman, the Staff, and that fuller constellation
is called Fruit Garland. Then, farther, nearing the pole:
Cradle, Path, the Burning Book, Doll, Window.
But in the southern sky, as clear as in the palm of a hand
blessed with the sign of the cross, that bright-shining M
which means the Mothers.". . . . . .

But the dead youth must depart, and in silence the elder
lament brings him up to the valley ravine,
where there's glimmering in the moonlight:
the wellspring of joy. Respectfully
she tells him the name of the spring, saying: "Among men
it's a carrying river."

They stand at the foot of the mountain range.
And then she embraces him, weeping.

Alone, he climbs up there, into the hills of primeval sorrow.
And not even his footfalls are audible in that soundless fate.

✿

But if the infinitely dead were to awaken a metaphor for us;
see: they might indicate the catkins of the empty
hazels, which hang down, or else
they might allude to the rain that falls on dark soil in spring. —

And we, who think of an *ascending*
happiness, would feel that emotion
which almost bewilders us
when a happy thing *falls*.

99. "Then a tree ascended. Oh, pure transcendence!"

Then a tree ascended. Oh, pure transcendence!
Oh, Orpheus sings! Oh, tall tree in the ear!
And all was silent. But even in that silencing
new beginnings, signs, and metamorphoses were at work.

Animals of silence forced their way out of the bright,
liberated forest, leaving lairs and nests;
and then it proved to be not out of cunning
or fear that they were so inwardly quiet,

but because they were listening. Roars, cries, bellows
seemed small in their hearts. And wherever

kaum eine Hütte war, dies zu empfangen,

ein Unterschlupf aus dunkelstem Verlangen
mit einem Zugang, dessen Pfosten beben,—
da schufst du ihnen Tempel im Gehör.

100. "Rühmen, das ists! Ein zum Rühmen Bestellter"

Rühmen, das ists! Ein zum Rühmen Bestellter,
ging er hervor wie das Erz aus des Steins
Schweigen. Sein Herz, o vergängliche Kelter
eines den Menschen unendlichen Weins.

Nie versagt ihm die Stimme am Staube,
wenn ihn das göttliche Beispiel ergreift.
Alles wird Weinberg, alles wird Traube,
in seinem fühlenden Süden gereift.

Nicht in den Grüften der Könige Moder
straft ihm die Rühmung lügen, oder
daß von den Göttern ein Schatten fällt.

Er ist einer der bleibenden Boten,
der noch weit in die Türen der Toten
Schalen mit rühmlichen Früchten hält.

101. "Nur wer die Leier schon hob"

Nur wer die Leier schon hob
auch unter Schatten,
darf das unendliche Lob
ahnend erstatten.

Nur wer mit Toten vom Mohn
aß, von dem ihren,
wird nicht den leisesten Ton
wieder verlieren.

Mag auch die Spieglung im Teich
oft uns verschwimmen:
Wisse das Bild.

Erst in dem Doppelbereich
werden die Stimmen
ewig und mild.

there had been barely a hut to receive this,

a hideaway formed out of darkest desire,
with an entryway whose posts were shaky—
you created temples for them in their ear.

100. "To praise, that's it! As one appointed to praise"

To praise, that's it! As one appointed to praise
he emerged like ore from the rock's
silence. His heart: oh, a mortal press
for a wine infinite to mankind!

His voice never fails him in the dust
when the divine example seizes him.
Everything becomes a vineyard, everything becomes grapes
ripened in the southland of his feelings.

The putrefaction of kings in tombs does not
give the lie to his praising, nor the fact
that a shadow falls from the gods.

He is one of the permanent messengers, one
who even far into the doors of the dead
holds bowls of the fruit of praise.

101. "Only the man who has already raised the lyre"

Only the man who has already raised the lyre,
even amid shadows,
is permitted to give infinite praise
with a presentiment.

Only the man who has eaten of the poppy
with the dead, of their poppy,
will no longer lose
the quietest sound.

Even if the reflection in the pool
often becomes blurred to us:
Know the image.

Only when one reaches the double realm
do the voices become
eternal and calm.

102. "Frühling ist wiedergekommen. Die Erde"

Frühling ist wiedergekommen. Die Erde
ist wie ein Kind, das Gedichte weiß;
viele, o viele. . . . Für die Beschwerde
langen Lernens bekommt sie den Preis.

Streng war ihr Lehrer. Wir mochten das Weiße
an dem Barte des alten Manns.
Nun, wie das Grüne, das Blaue heiße,
dürfen wir fragen: sie kanns, sie kanns!

Erde, die frei hat, du glückliche, spiele
nun mit den Kindern. Wir wollen dich fangen,
fröhliche Erde. Dem Frohsten gelingts.

O, was der Lehrer sie lehrte, das Viele,
und was gedruckt steht in Wurzeln und langen
schwierigen Stämmen: sie singts, sie singts!

103. "Wolle die Wandlung. O sei für die Flamme begeistert"

Wolle die Wandlung. O sei für die Flamme begeistert,
drin sich ein Ding dir entzieht, das mit Verwandlungen prunkt;
jener entwerfende Geist, welcher das Irdische meistert,
liebt in dem Schwung der Figur nichts wie den wendenden Punkt.

Was sich ins Bleiben verschließt, schon *ists* das Erstarrte;
wähnt es sich sicher im Schutz des unscheinbaren Grau's?
Warte, ein Härtestes warnt aus der Ferne das Harte.
Wehe—: abwesender Hammer holt aus!

Wer sich als Quelle ergießt, den erkennt die Erkennung;
und sie führt ihn entzückt durch das heiter Geschaffne,
das mit Anfang oft schließt und mit Ende beginnt.

Jeder glückliche Raum ist Kind oder Enkel von Trennung,
den sie staunend durchgehn. Und die verwandelte Daphne
will, seit sie lorbeern fühlt, daß du dich wandelst in Wind.

102. "Spring has returned. The earth"

Spring has returned. The earth
is like a child that knows poems;
many, oh, many. . . . For the trouble
of loyng learning she's receiving a reward.

Her teacher was strict. We liked the white
in the old fellow's beard.
Now we're allowed to ask the names
of that green, that blue: she knows them, she knows!

Earth, you that are on holiday, happy one, now
play with the children! We want to catch you,
merry earth. The most joyous one will succeed.

Oh, all those things her teacher taught her,
things printed in roots and long,
difficult stems: she sings them, she sings!

103. "Desire transformation! Oh, be enthusiastic for the flame"

Desire transformation! Oh, be enthusiastic for the flame
in which a thing that flaunts its transformations eludes you;
that planning spirit which masters earthly matters
loves nothing so much in the swing of the figure as the point that turns.

That which locks itself into permanence *is* already rigid;
does it imagine it's safe under the protection of inconspicuous gray?
Wait: from afar something very hard warns what is hard.
Woe! an absent hammer is raised for the blow!

The man who pours himself out like a spring is known by knowledge,
which delightedly leads him through that which has been joyously created,
and which often ends with its start and starts with its end.

Every happy space is the child or grandchild of separation,
the space they traverse in amazement. And Daphne transformed,
ever since she has felt like a laurel, has wanted you to change into wind.

104. "Singe die Gärten, mein Herz . . ."

Singe die Gärten, mein Herz, die du nicht kennst; wie in Glas
eingegossene Gärten, klar, unerreichbar.
Wasser und Rosen von Ispahan oder Schiras,
singe sie selig, preise sie, keinem vergleichbar.

Zeige, mein Herz, daß du sie niemals entbehrst.
Daß sie dich meinen, ihre reifenden Feigen.
Daß du mit ihren, zwischen den blühenden Zweigen
wie zum Gesicht gesteigerten Lüften verkehrst.

Meide den Irrtum, daß es Entbehrungen gebe
für den geschehnen Entschluß, diesen: zu sein!
Seidener Faden, kamst du hinein ins Gewebe.

Welchem der Bilder du auch im Innern geeint bist
(sei es selbst ein Moment aus dem Leben der Pein),
fühl, daß der ganze, der rühmliche Teppich gemeint ist.

104. "Sing the gardens, my heart . . ."

Sing the gardens, my heart, that you don't know; gardens
as if molded in glass, bright, unattainable.
Water and roses from Ispahan or Shiraz:
sing them blissfully, praise them, comparable to none.

Show, my heart, that you're never deprived of them.
That their ripening figs are meant for you.
That you're conversant with their breezes, which are heightened
as if to vision among the blossoming boughs.

Avoid the mistaken view that there exist deprivations
for the decision that has been taken, the decision to be!
You have entered the woven fabric as a silken thread.

To whichever of the images you are inwardly united
(be it even a moment in the life of sorrow),
feel that the entire carpet of praise is intended.

ALPHABETICAL LIST OF GERMAN TITLES

ALPHABETICAL LIST OF GERMAN FIRST LINES

A CATALOG OF SELECTED
DOVER BOOKS
IN ALL FIELDS OF INTEREST

A CATALOG OF SELECTED DOVER
BOOKS IN ALL FIELDS OF INTEREST

100 BEST-LOVED POEMS, Edited by Philip Smith. "The Passionate Shepherd to His Love," "Shall I compare thee to a summer's day?" "Death, be not proud," "The Raven," "The Road Not Taken," plus works by Blake, Wordsworth, Byron, Shelley, Keats, many others. 96pp. 5³⁄₁₆ x 8¼. 0-486-28553-7

100 SMALL HOUSES OF THE THIRTIES, Brown-Blodgett Company. Exterior photographs and floor plans for 100 charming structures. Illustrations of models accompanied by descriptions of interiors, color schemes, closet space, and other amenities. 200 illustrations. 112pp. 8⅜ x 11. 0-486-44131-8

1000 TURN-OF-THE-CENTURY HOUSES: With Illustrations and Floor Plans, Herbert C. Chivers. Reproduced from a rare edition, this showcase of homes ranges from cottages and bungalows to sprawling mansions. Each house is meticulously illustrated and accompanied by complete floor plans. 256pp. 9⅜ x 12¼.
0-486-45596-3

101 GREAT AMERICAN POEMS, Edited by The American Poetry & Literacy Project. Rich treasury of verse from the 19th and 20th centuries includes works by Edgar Allan Poe, Robert Frost, Walt Whitman, Langston Hughes, Emily Dickinson, T. S. Eliot, other notables. 96pp. 5³⁄₁₆ x 8¼. 0-486-40158-8

101 GREAT SAMURAI PRINTS, Utagawa Kuniyoshi. Kuniyoshi was a master of the warrior woodblock print — and these 18th-century illustrations represent the pinnacle of his craft. Full-color portraits of renowned Japanese samurais pulse with movement, passion, and remarkably fine detail. 112pp. 8⅜ x 11. 0-486-46523-3

ABC OF BALLET, Janet Grosser. Clearly worded, abundantly illustrated little guide defines basic ballet-related terms: arabesque, battement, pas de chat, relevé, sissonne, many others. Pronunciation guide included. Excellent primer. 48pp. 4³⁄₁₆ x 5¾.
0-486-40871-X

ACCESSORIES OF DRESS: An Illustrated Encyclopedia, Katherine Lester and Bess Viola Oerke. Illustrations of hats, veils, wigs, cravats, shawls, shoes, gloves, and other accessories enhance an engaging commentary that reveals the humor and charm of the many-sided story of accessorized apparel. 644 figures and 59 plates. 608pp. 6⅛ x 9¼.
0-486-43378-1

ADVENTURES OF HUCKLEBERRY FINN, Mark Twain. Join Huck and Jim as their boyhood adventures along the Mississippi River lead them into a world of excitement, danger, and self-discovery. Humorous narrative, lyrical descriptions of the Mississippi valley, and memorable characters. 224pp. 5³⁄₁₆ x 8¼. 0-486-28061-6

ALICE STARMORE'S BOOK OF FAIR ISLE KNITTING, Alice Starmore. A noted designer from the region of Scotland's Fair Isle explores the history and techniques of this distinctive, stranded-color knitting style and provides copious illustrated instructions for 14 original knitwear designs. 208pp. 8⅜ x 10⅞. 0-486-47218-3

Browse over 9,000 books at www.doverpublications.com

CATALOG OF DOVER BOOKS

ALICE'S ADVENTURES IN WONDERLAND, Lewis Carroll. Beloved classic about a little girl lost in a topsy-turvy land and her encounters with the White Rabbit, March Hare, Mad Hatter, Cheshire Cat, and other delightfully improbable characters. 42 illustrations by Sir John Tenniel. 96pp. 5³⁄₁₆ x 8¼.   0-486-27543-4

AMERICA'S LIGHTHOUSES: An Illustrated History, Francis Ross Holland. Profusely illustrated fact-filled survey of American lighthouses since 1716. Over 200 stations — East, Gulf, and West coasts, Great Lakes, Hawaii, Alaska, Puerto Rico, the Virgin Islands, and the Mississippi and St. Lawrence Rivers. 240pp. 8 x 10¾.
0-486-25576-X

AN ENCYCLOPEDIA OF THE VIOLIN, Alberto Bachmann. Translated by Frederick H. Martens. Introduction by Eugene Ysaye. First published in 1925, this renowned reference remains unsurpassed as a source of essential information, from construction and evolution to repertoire and technique. Includes a glossary and 73 illustrations. 496pp. 6⅛ x 9¼.   0-486-46618-3

ANIMALS: 1,419 Copyright-Free Illustrations of Mammals, Birds, Fish, Insects, etc., Selected by Jim Harter. Selected for its visual impact and ease of use, this outstanding collection of wood engravings presents over 1,000 species of animals in extremely lifelike poses. Includes mammals, birds, reptiles, amphibians, fish, insects, and other invertebrates. 284pp. 9 x 12.   0-486-23766-4

THE ANNALS, Tacitus. Translated by Alfred John Church and William Jackson Brodribb. This vital chronicle of Imperial Rome, written by the era's great historian, spans A.D. 14-68 and paints incisive psychological portraits of major figures, from Tiberius to Nero. 416pp. 5³⁄₁₆ x 8¼.   0-486-45236-0

ANTIGONE, Sophocles. Filled with passionate speeches and sensitive probing of moral and philosophical issues, this powerful and often-performed Greek drama reveals the grim fate that befalls the children of Oedipus. Footnotes. 64pp. 5³⁄₁₆ x 8 ¼.   0-486-27804-2

ART DECO DECORATIVE PATTERNS IN FULL COLOR, Christian Stoll. Reprinted from a rare 1910 portfolio, 160 sensuous and exotic images depict a breathtaking array of florals, geometrics, and abstracts — all elegant in their stark simplicity. 64pp. 8⅜ x 11.   0-486-44862-2

THE ARTHUR RACKHAM TREASURY: 86 Full-Color Illustrations, Arthur Rackham. Selected and Edited by Jeff A. Menges. A stunning treasury of 86 full-page plates span the famed English artist's career, from *Rip Van Winkle* (1905) to masterworks such as *Undine, A Midsummer Night's Dream,* and *Wind in the Willows* (1939). 96pp. 8⅜ x 11.
0-486-44685-9

THE AUTHENTIC GILBERT & SULLIVAN SONGBOOK, W. S. Gilbert and A. S. Sullivan. The most comprehensive collection available, this songbook includes selections from every one of Gilbert and Sullivan's light operas. Ninety-two numbers are presented uncut and unedited, and in their original keys. 410pp. 9 x 12.
0-486-23482-7

THE AWAKENING, Kate Chopin. First published in 1899, this controversial novel of a New Orleans wife's search for love outside a stifling marriage shocked readers. Today, it remains a first-rate narrative with superb characterization. New introductory Note. 128pp. 5³⁄₁₆ x 8¼.   0-486-27786-0

BASIC DRAWING, Louis Priscilla. Beginning with perspective, this commonsense manual progresses to the figure in movement, light and shade, anatomy, drapery, composition, trees and landscape, and outdoor sketching. Black-and-white illustrations throughout. 128pp. 8⅜ x 11.   0-486-45815-6

Browse over 9,000 books at www.doverpublications.com

THE BATTLES THAT CHANGED HISTORY, Fletcher Pratt. Historian profiles 16 crucial conflicts, ancient to modern, that changed the course of Western civilization. Gripping accounts of battles led by Alexander the Great, Joan of Arc, Ulysses S. Grant, other commanders. 27 maps. 352pp. 5⅜ x 8½.   0-486-41129-X

BEETHOVEN'S LETTERS, Ludwig van Beethoven. Edited by Dr. A. C. Kalischer. Features 457 letters to fellow musicians, friends, greats, patrons, and literary men. Reveals musical thoughts, quirks of personality, insights, and daily events. Includes 15 plates. 410pp. 5⅜ x 8½.   0-486-22769-3

BERNICE BOBS HER HAIR AND OTHER STORIES, F. Scott Fitzgerald. This brilliant anthology includes 6 of Fitzgerald's most popular stories: "The Diamond as Big as the Ritz," the title tale, "The Offshore Pirate," "The Ice Palace," "The Jelly Bean," and "May Day." 176pp. 5⅜ x 8½.   0-486-47049-0

BESLER'S BOOK OF FLOWERS AND PLANTS: 73 Full-Color Plates from Hortus Eystettensis, 1613, Basilius Besler. Here is a selection of magnificent plates from the *Hortus Eystettensis,* which vividly illustrated and identified the plants, flowers, and trees that thrived in the legendary German garden at Eichstätt. 80pp. 8⅜ x 11.
                0-486-46005-3

THE BOOK OF KELLS, Edited by Blanche Cirker. Painstakingly reproduced from a rare facsimile edition, this volume contains full-page decorations, portraits, illustrations, plus a sampling of textual leaves with exquisite calligraphy and ornamentation. 32 full-color illustrations. 32pp. 9⅜ x 12¼.   0-486-24345-1

THE BOOK OF THE CROSSBOW: With an Additional Section on Catapults and Other Siege Engines, Ralph Payne-Gallwey. Fascinating study traces history and use of crossbow as military and sporting weapon, from Middle Ages to modern times. Also covers related weapons: balistas, catapults, Turkish bows, more. Over 240 illustrations. 400pp. 7¼ x 10⅛.   0-486-28720-3

THE BUNGALOW BOOK: Floor Plans and Photos of 112 Houses, 1910, Henry L. Wilson. Here are 112 of the most popular and economic blueprints of the early 20th century — plus an illustration or photograph of each completed house. A wonderful time capsule that still offers a wealth of valuable insights. 160pp. 8⅜ x 11.
                0-486-45104-6

THE CALL OF THE WILD, Jack London. A classic novel of adventure, drawn from London's own experiences as a Klondike adventurer, relating the story of a heroic dog caught in the brutal life of the Alaska Gold Rush. Note. 64pp. 5³⁄₁₆ x 8¼.
                0-486-26472-6

CANDIDE, Voltaire. Edited by Francois-Marie Arouet. One of the world's great satires since its first publication in 1759. Witty, caustic skewering of romance, science, philosophy, religion, government — nearly all human ideals and institutions. 112pp. 5³⁄₁₆ x 8¼.   0-486-26689-3

CELEBRATED IN THEIR TIME: Photographic Portraits from the George Grantham Bain Collection, Edited by Amy Pastan. With an Introduction by Michael Carlebach. Remarkable portrait gallery features 112 rare images of Albert Einstein, Charlie Chaplin, the Wright Brothers, Henry Ford, and other luminaries from the worlds of politics, art, entertainment, and industry. 128pp. 8⅜ x 11.   0-486-46754-6

CHARIOTS FOR APOLLO: The NASA History of Manned Lunar Spacecraft to 1969, Courtney G. Brooks, James M. Grimwood, and Loyd S. Swenson, Jr. This illustrated history by a trio of experts is the definitive reference on the Apollo spacecraft and lunar modules. It traces the vehicles' design, development, and operation in space. More than 100 photographs and illustrations. 576pp. 6¾ x 9¼. 0-486-46756-2

Browse over 9,000 books at www.doverpublications.com

A CHRISTMAS CAROL, Charles Dickens. This engrossing tale relates Ebenezer Scrooge's ghostly journeys through Christmases past, present, and future and his ultimate transformation from a harsh and grasping old miser to a charitable and compassionate human being. 80pp. 5³⁄₁₆ x 8¼.　　　　0-486-26865-9

COMMON SENSE, Thomas Paine. First published in January of 1776, this highly influential landmark document clearly and persuasively argued for American separation from Great Britain and paved the way for the Declaration of Independence. 64pp. 5³⁄₁₆ x 8¼.　　　　0-486-29602-4

THE COMPLETE SHORT STORIES OF OSCAR WILDE, Oscar Wilde. Complete texts of "The Happy Prince and Other Tales," "A House of Pomegranates," "Lord Arthur Savile's Crime and Other Stories," "Poems in Prose," and "The Portrait of Mr. W. H." 208pp. 5³⁄₁₆ x 8¼.　　　　0-486-45216-6

COMPLETE SONNETS, William Shakespeare. Over 150 exquisite poems deal with love, friendship, the tyranny of time, beauty's evanescence, death, and other themes in language of remarkable power, precision, and beauty. Glossary of archaic terms. 80pp. 5³⁄₁₆ x 8¼.　　　　0-486-26686-9

THE COUNT OF MONTE CRISTO: Abridged Edition, Alexandre Dumas. Falsely accused of treason, Edmond Dantès is imprisoned in the bleak Chateau d'If. After a hair-raising escape, he launches an elaborate plot to extract a bitter revenge against those who betrayed him. 448pp. 5³⁄₁₆ x 8¼.　　　　0-486-45643-9

CRAFTSMAN BUNGALOWS: Designs from the Pacific Northwest, Yoho & Merritt. This reprint of a rare catalog, showcasing the charming simplicity and cozy style of Craftsman bungalows, is filled with photos of completed homes, plus floor plans and estimated costs. An indispensable resource for architects, historians, and illustrators. 112pp. 10 x 7.　　　　0-486-46875-5

CRAFTSMAN BUNGALOWS: 59 Homes from "The Craftsman," Edited by Gustav Stickley. Best and most attractive designs from Arts and Crafts Movement publication — 1903–1916 — includes sketches, photographs of homes, floor plans, descriptive text. 128pp. 8¼ x 11.　　　　0-486-25829-7

CRIME AND PUNISHMENT, Fyodor Dostoyevsky. Translated by Constance Garnett. Supreme masterpiece tells the story of Raskolnikov, a student tormented by his own thoughts after he murders an old woman. Overwhelmed by guilt and terror, he confesses and goes to prison. 480pp. 5³⁄₁₆ x 8¼.　　　　0-486-41587-2

THE DECLARATION OF INDEPENDENCE AND OTHER GREAT DOCUMENTS OF AMERICAN HISTORY: 1775-1865, Edited by John Grafton. Thirteen compelling and influential documents: Henry's "Give Me Liberty or Give Me Death," Declaration of Independence, The Constitution, Washington's First Inaugural Address, The Monroe Doctrine, The Emancipation Proclamation, Gettysburg Address, more. 64pp. 5³⁄₁₆ x 8¼.　　　　0-486-41124-9

THE DESERT AND THE SOWN: Travels in Palestine and Syria, Gertrude Bell. "The female Lawrence of Arabia," Gertrude Bell wrote captivating, perceptive accounts of her travels in the Middle East. This intriguing narrative, accompanied by 160 photos, traces her 1905 sojourn in Lebanon, Syria, and Palestine. 368pp. 5⅜ x 8½.　　　　0-486-46876-3

A DOLL'S HOUSE, Henrik Ibsen. Ibsen's best-known play displays his genius for realistic prose drama. An expression of women's rights, the play climaxes when the central character, Nora, rejects a smothering marriage and life in "a doll's house." 80pp. 5³⁄₁₆ x 8¼.　　　　0-486-27062-9

Browse over 9,000 books at www.doverpublications.com

DOOMED SHIPS: Great Ocean Liner Disasters, William H. Miller, Jr. Nearly 200 photographs, many from private collections, highlight tales of some of the vessels whose pleasure cruises ended in catastrophe: the *Morro Castle, Normandie, Andrea Doria, Europa,* and many others. 128pp. 8⅜ x 11¼.   0-486-45366-9

THE DORÉ BIBLE ILLUSTRATIONS, Gustave Doré. Detailed plates from the Bible: the Creation scenes, Adam and Eve, horrifying visions of the Flood, the battle sequences with their monumental crowds, depictions of the life of Jesus, 241 plates in all. 241pp. 9 x 12.   0-486-23004-X

DRAWING DRAPERY FROM HEAD TO TOE, Cliff Young. Expert guidance on how to draw shirts, pants, skirts, gloves, hats, and coats on the human figure, including folds in relation to the body, pull and crush, action folds, creases, more. Over 200 drawings. 48pp. 8¼ x 11.   0-486-45591-2

DUBLINERS, James Joyce. A fine and accessible introduction to the work of one of the 20th century's most influential writers, this collection features 15 tales, including a masterpiece of the short-story genre, "The Dead." 160pp. 5³⁄₁₆ x 8¼.
0-486-26870-5

EASY-TO-MAKE POP-UPS, Joan Irvine. Illustrated by Barbara Reid. Dozens of wonderful ideas for three-dimensional paper fun — from holiday greeting cards with moving parts to a pop-up menagerie. Easy-to-follow, illustrated instructions for more than 30 projects. 299 black-and-white illustrations. 96pp. 8⅜ x 11.
0-486-44622-0

EASY-TO-MAKE STORYBOOK DOLLS: A "Novel" Approach to Cloth Dollmaking, Sherralyn St. Clair. Favorite fictional characters come alive in this unique beginner's dollmaking guide. Includes patterns for Pollyanna, Dorothy from *The Wonderful Wizard of Oz,* Mary of *The Secret Garden,* plus easy-to-follow instructions, 263 black-and-white illustrations, and an 8-page color insert. 112pp. 8¼ x 11.   0-486-47360-0

EINSTEIN'S ESSAYS IN SCIENCE, Albert Einstein. Speeches and essays in accessible, everyday language profile influential physicists such as Niels Bohr and Isaac Newton. They also explore areas of physics to which the author made major contributions. 128pp. 5 x 8.   0-486-47011-3

EL DORADO: Further Adventures of the Scarlet Pimpernel, Baroness Orczy. A popular sequel to *The Scarlet Pimpernel,* this suspenseful story recounts the Pimpernel's attempts to rescue the Dauphin from imprisonment during the French Revolution. An irresistible blend of intrigue, period detail, and vibrant characterizations. 352pp. 5³⁄₁₆ x 8¼.   0-486-44026-5

ELEGANT SMALL HOMES OF THE TWENTIES: 99 Designs from a Competition, Chicago Tribune. Nearly 100 designs for five- and six-room houses feature New England and Southern colonials, Normandy cottages, stately Italianate dwellings, and other fascinating snapshots of American domestic architecture of the 1920s. 112pp. 9 x 12.   0-486-46910-7

THE ELEMENTS OF STYLE: The Original Edition, William Strunk, Jr. This is the book that generations of writers have relied upon for timeless advice on grammar, diction, syntax, and other essentials. In concise terms, it identifies the principal requirements of proper style and common errors. 64pp. 5⅜ x 8½.   0-486-44798-7

THE ELUSIVE PIMPERNEL, Baroness Orczy. Robespierre's revolutionaries find their wicked schemes thwarted by the heroic Pimpernel — Sir Percival Blakeney. In this thrilling sequel, Chauvelin devises a plot to eliminate the Pimpernel and his wife. 272pp. 5³⁄₁₆ x 8¼.   0-486-45464-9

Browse over 9,000 books at www.doverpublications.com